YOUR
REPTILE
PET

YOUR
REPTILE
PET

Richard Headstrom

David McKay Company, Inc.
New York

ILLUSTRATION CREDITS

Line drawings by the author
Ross Allen, St. Augustine Alligator Farm, Inc., St. Augustine, Florida, pages 70, 76
(bottom), 88, 102; Animals Animals, New York, page 60; Chicago Natural History
Museum, page 100; Courtesy, Field Museum of Natural History, Chicago, pages 44, 46,
48, 54, 58, 66, 74, 76 (top), 80 (top), 84, 90, 92, 94, 96, 102 (top), 107; San Diego Zoo
photo, page 52.

Library of Congress Cataloging in Publication Data
Headstrom, Birger Richard, 1902-
Your reptile pet.
Bibliography: p.117
Includes index.
SUMMARY: Discusses the characteristics and habits of a variety of
reptiles including turtles, anoles, lizards, snakes, and caymans
and suggests ways to care for reptile pets.
1. Reptiles as pets—Juvenile literature.
[1. Reptiles as pets] I. Title.
SF459.R4H4   639'.39   78-4414
ISBN 9-679-21100-4

1 2 3 4 5 6 7 8 9 10
Manufactured in the United States of America

To John

Contents

Introduction

What kind of animals are reptiles? Reptiles are cold-blooded, back-boned animals that breathe by means of lungs. They are usually covered with scales, frequently with bony plates. The word reptile comes from the Latin word *repere*, to crawl or creep. Reptiles are creeping or crawling animals, though some of them, like the lizards, can run over the ground quite rapidly.

THE PLACE OF REPTILES IN THE ANIMAL KINGDOM

All matter, living (organic) and non-living (inorganic), is divided for purposes of classification into three great kingdoms: mineral, plant, and animal. (Some scientists have added a fourth, the synthetic kingdom, which includes substances or products developed from the other three.) The animal kingdom includes all living forms that move freely, take in food, grow, and reproduce. It is divided into a number of large divisions called phyla (singular phylum). The phyla, in turn, are divided into smaller divisions called the classes, the classes into orders, the orders into families, and the families into genera which are made up of species. All animals are classified according to structure, therefore all the animals belonging to a phylum, class, order, and so on have certain structural characteristics in common.

Reptiles belong to the class Reptilia, which includes turtles, tortoises, lizards, snakes, crocodiles, alligators, gavials, caimans, and the tuatara, a lizardlike reptile found only in New Zealand. If we were to classify a reptile, such as the common garter snake, we would proceed as follows:

1

                Phylum *Chordata*
                Subphylum *Vertebrata*
                Class *Reptilia*
                Order *Squamata*
                Suborder *Serpentes*
                Family *Colubridae*
                Genus *Thamnophis*
                Species *sirtalis*
                Subspecies *sirtalis*

The scientific name of the common garter snake, or more specifically the eastern garter snake, is *Thamnophis sirtalis sirtalis*.

THE ORIGIN OF REPTILES

Lizards, turtles, and crocodiles are said to have descended from the so-called stem-reptiles or cotylosaurs, primitive reptiles that developed from amphibians that flourished during the late Devonian and Triassic times. They have been on the earth for some 2,000,000,000 years. Snakes are believed to have evolved from the lizards we know as monitors. There have been snakes on earth since the Cretaceous period, or for at least 100,000,000 years.

MYTHS, MYTHOLOGY, AND FOLKLORE

The Book of Rites, a classic of ancient China, listed the tortoise as one of the four benevolent spiritual animals, and for centuries the Chinese have regarded the tortoise as an emblem of longevity and a symbol of righteousness. The ancient Hindus believed the earth to be a hemisphere with its flat side resting on the backs of four elephants that in turn stood on a huge turtle. The Greeks believed that the turtle was sacred to the god Pan. Many American Indians venerated the turtle and made ceremonial rattles from its shell. The story of the hare and the tortoise has made the tortoise a symbol of plodding determination.

So much misinformation about snakes has developed over the centuries that these animals have come to be universally loathed, maligned, and even feared. It is widely believed that all snakes are poisonous, slimy, sting with their tongues, and charm their prey—all of which is quite untrue. It is also believed that a snake that has been killed will be avenged by its mate; that the

2

age of a rattlesnake can be determined from the number of its rattles; and that whiskey is a cure for snakebite. There are stories about snakes sucking milk from cows and of mother snakes swallowing their young when they are threatened with danger. It is said that glass snakes fly to pieces when struck and then later reassemble their parts, and that the hoop snake takes its tail in its mouth and rolls like a hoop. There even is a North American fable about a snake that blows a deadly, or at least harmful, poison.

It is widely believed that many lizards are highly venomous, though only two species are poisonous: the Gila monster and the Mexican beaded lizard. In the southeastern United States, the large red-headed males of the blue-tailed skink are thought to be very dangerous because of their potent venom, but they are entirely harmless and quickly hide upon seeing a human.

A bit of folklore concerning the alligator and the crocodile dates back to ancient Greece. This is the belief that the two animals can be distinguished by the way in which they open their mouths. The alligator is said to open its mouth by moving the lower jaw and the crocodile by raising its upper jaw. Like most vertebrates, both the alligator and crocodile open their mouths the same way, by moving only the lower jaw.

ABUNDANCE AND DISTRIBUTION OF REPTILES

There are some 250 species of turtles found throughout the warmer regions of the world. Being cold-blooded, they cannot survive in places that are permanently frozen. Land and freshwater turtles are abundant on all continents but Europe. Rich turtle faunas occur in Africa, eastern North America and southeastern Asia. Only six species are listed for Europe and five of these are found in other continents; the British Isles do not have any turtles. Sea turtles occur throughout tropical and subtropical regions but breed largely within the tropics. They often wander into temperate seas or are carried there by currents.

There are more than 2,500 species of snakes today. Like the turtles they are found only in the warmer parts of the world. One species, however, reaches the Arctic Circle in Scandinavia where the Gulf Stream modifies the climate. In Eurasia, snakes are found northward to a latitude several degrees below the Arctic Circle. In North America they thrive as far north as Hudson Bay, and in South America at the extreme tip of the continent. The marine species—sea snakes—range from southern Japan southeastward as far as the Samoan Islands and westward along the Asiatic coasts to the Persian Gulf. One marine species has reached the western coast of the New World and the eastern coast of Africa.

There are approximately 2,700 species of lizards. Like the turtles and snakes they are found only in the warmer parts of the world. They occur on all the continents and on many oceanic islands where there is no other reptile life. A species of European lizard is found as far north as the Arctic Circle. In North America only four species are found in Canada, and these live in the southernmost parts.

There are two species of alligators, the American and the Chinese, and some twenty-one species of crocodiles, which are typically animals of the tropics and subtropics. The American alligator is found in the southeastern part of the United States; the Chinese alligator only in China. Crocodiles are distributed from Africa and Madagascar throughout the Pacific (New Guinea, the Philippines, southern Asia, and the Malay Archipelago), and in Central America, the West Indies, and South America. The five species of caimans, are found from the Isthmus of Tehuantepec in southern Mexico to northern Argentina.

THE AGE OF REPTILES

It is generally believed that turtles live an incredibly long time, but this is a fallacy. While they undoubtedly live longer than other backboned animals, there is no evidence that they live hundreds of years. Records of the life span of turtles are all based on captive specimens and show that a few species may live well over a century. Longevity records of snakes are also based on captive specimens and indicate that snakes can live in captivity for twenty years or more. The potential life span of a snake seems to be between twenty to thirty years.

Most of our knowledge about the life span of lizards also comes from those kept in captivity. A Gila monster has been known to have lived for about twenty years in captivity, but the maximum age of most North American lizards in their natural surroundings is probably eight or nine years. A study of the fence swift done in Florida, where the lizard is active throughout the

4

year, showed that ninety-four per cent of these lizards lived less than a year, and none lived for two years. But in Maryland, where the lizard is active for only seven months of the year, the fence swift lives for more than four years and probably as long as eight years.

Despite the claims of an alligator farm in Florida that some of its inhabitants might be approaching 1,000, the maximum age definitely known for an American alligator is fifty-six years. It is also known that a Chinese alligator lived for fifty years and a marsh crocodile for thirty-one years. When these records were made, all three reptiles were still alive, but so far there is no evidence that crocodilians live even as long as human beings.

THE SIZE OF REPTILES

Turtles range in size from a few inches to several feet. The shell length of the striped and common mud turtles, for example, averages between three and four inches, while the overall length of the leatherback turtle may be as much as nine feet. The leatherback turtle weighs up to three-quarters of a ton (1,500 pounds) and the yellow mud turtle about thirteen ounces.

Snakes range in length from a few inches, (nine to thirteen inches for the brown snake), to as much as thirty-two feet (reticulate python of Asia). The king cobra, with a maximum known length of eighteen feet and four inches, is by far the largest venomous snake. The eastern diamond-back snake may very well be the heaviest of all snakes.

Like the turtles, the lizards range from a few inches in size to as much as the ten feet reached by the Komodo dragon. Next in size is the common iguana of the American tropics that reaches a length of six feet, seven inches. The largest lizard in the United States is the glass lizard whose usual length is slightly less than three feet. (A record is forty-two and six-tenths inches); the Gila monster measures about two feet. The smallest lizard, the gecko is only one and one-third inches long.

Crocodiles range in size from three feet (Congo dwarf crocodile) to twelve feet (salt-water crocodile). The American crocodile averages between ten to twelve feet, though an American crocodile has measured as much as twenty-three feet. The American alligator usually averages between eight to ten feet in length, its greatest length being nineteen and one-sixth feet.

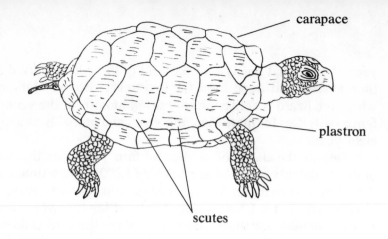

carapace

plastron

scutes

Fig. 1   External view of turtle

THE EXTERNAL FEATURES OF REPTILES

Outer Covering

Turtles are unique. They are the only animals that have a shell as an outer covering. The shell is broad and flattened and consists of a convex upper part called the carapace (Fig. 1) and a lower flattened part called the plastron (Fig. 1). Both parts are strongly held together on each side by bony bridges that vary in width with the species. The shell is usually covered with a number of symmetrically arranged horny plates known as scutes (shields). The number and shape of the scutes vary according to the species and are usually similar in individuals of the same species (Fig. 1). Soft-shelled turtles have a leathery shell that is not divided into scutes and contains little bony material. The skin of turtles is thin and smooth on the head, but thick, tough, scaly, and very wrinkled over the exposed parts of the body such as the neck and legs.

The outer covering, or skin, of snakes is covered with dry, horny scales. The scales on the head are usually so regular that scientists can use them in classifying snakes. These scales are almost always enlarged and are different from those on the rest of the animal's body. They are called head shields or head plates (Fig. 2). The upper or dorsal scales are longer than they are wide. They are arranged both in straight longitudinal rows and in diagonal rows across the body. The number of rows often varies on different parts of the body, according to the amount of tapering (Fig. 2). The dorsal scales may be keeled or smooth (Fig. 3). Snakes with keeled dorsal scales sometimes have one or more smooth lateral rows. With the exception of the blind snakes, all North American snakes have ventral plates, or ventrals, which

6

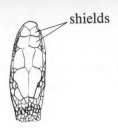

Fig. 2 Top of head of snake

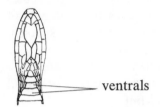

ventrals

Fig. 3 keeled scale smooth scale

Fig. 4 Underside of head of snake

extend from side to side (Fig. 4) on the lower surface of the body. In many snakes the ventrals extend onto the sides of the body. When they turn upward with a more or less abrupt angle they are said to be angularly bent.

The external covering of lizards consists of a dry skin covered with scales which vary greatly in form. Like the scales of snakes they are of value in classifying lizards. The thick leathery skin of crocodiles and alligators is covered with horny epidermal scales, and with dorsal and sometimes ventral bony plates somewhat like those in the shell of the turtles. The horny scales are set in rows and have keels that form continuous ridges. The resulting armor is so tough that it might be described as impenetrable. The animal's massive skull is so bony that it presents no vulnerable spot.

As the skin of snakes and lizards is inelastic and cannot stretch, it must be shed periodically to enable the animals to grow. This shedding process is called molting. Snakes molt by shedding the outermost layer of skin (the cuticle) that has been replaced by a new layer of cuticle that develops beneath it. About ten days or so before a snake sheds its skin, its eyes become milky and assume a bluish opacity, and the snake is then blind. It also loses its appetite. The colors on the body become so dull that the animal has a drab and dirty appearance. About a week before molting the eyes clear, and the snake can see again.

The old layer of skin begins to loosen about the head. By rubbing its head against stones, shrubbery or other objects, the snake works the skin back, turning it inside out. By the action of wavelike muscular contractions and by rubbing its body against such objects as are available, the snake gradually strips the skin back over its body. As the skin peels off, it turns inside out like a stocking that is grasped at the top and pulled off by turning it wrong side out.

The snake usually sheds its skin in one piece. It can do this because the folds that extend down between the scales flatten out as the skin peels off. This increases the diameter of the skin.

The way lizards molt varies with the species. The soft-skinned or granular-skinned species shed in very large pieces. The larger and rough-scaled lizards shed scale by scale. Some lizards shed over the entire body, whereas others do so separately on the head, body and tail.

As with the snakes, before the old skin is shed, a new one forms beneath it. When the old skin is shed, the new one is shiny, and the markings and colors are quite vivid. In time these fade as another skin forms beneath it.

The shedding of the outer skin is not a simple process, because the parts of the lizard's head are not movable and the skin is closely attached to the eyes, ears, lips, and nostrils. Lizards have developed a swell mechanism by which they can increase the blood pressure in the veins of the head causing the head to expand. This swelling has the effect of loosening the skin so that the lizard can remove it by rubbing its body against an object, or by scratching it with one of its feet.

The Head

In turtles, the head is flattened on both the upper and lower surfaces. In snakes, the size and breadth of the head varies in the different species. The head of blind snakes and of many other burrowing forms is no wider than the body of the neck. In rattlesnakes and pit vipers the head is wide enough to allow for enlarged poison glands. The head of the lizards varies in size and shape according to the species, and in the crocodiles and alligators it is extended into a long bony snout.

The Mouth

A turtle's mouth is rather large. A snake can extend its mouth to permit it to swallow food many times its own size. A snake's lower jaw is connected very loosely to the skull by means of two slender bones, or quadrates. The lower jaw is also separated into two halves connected by an elastic ligament that

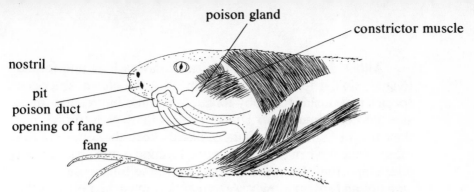

Fig. 5 Head of rattlesnake showing fangs, poison gland, and poison duct

enables them to be spread apart at the anterior midpoint. The toothbearing bones of the upper jaw are independently movable (Fig. 5). Most snakes have a longitudinal groove, the mental groove, beneath the chin. This mental groove is bordered by enlarged scales that permit the skin to expand when the jaws are spread. In the crocodiles and alligators the powerful jaws are extended into the long snout.

The Teeth

Turtles do not have any teeth. They crush their food with horny plates that form the margins of the jaws. Snakes have sharp teeth that curve inward. The curved teeth prevent food from slipping forward when the snake has begun to swallow. In the venomous snakes certain teeth are grooved or tubular and conduct venom into any animal the snake has bitten (Fig. 5).

Most lizards have teeth that are usually conical in shape and are arranged in a single row along the edges of the jaws. Lizards also have an extraordinary dental adaptation called the egg tooth. An egg tooth is a very sharp-edged centrally placed tooth that projects forward from the upper lip in the embryo. At the time of hatching, it is used to slit open the shell to help the young lizard to emerge from the egg. The young lizard sheds the egg tooth soon after hatching. Both the crocodiles and alligators have numerous conical teeth that are set in bony sockets.

The Tongue

The tongue of turtles is broad and soft and is attached to the floor of the mouth cavity. It is not protrusible, that is, it cannot be thrust forward. The tongue of a snake is a long, narrow, deeply forked, protrusible organ. It can be extended out even when the mouth is closed through grooves in the snake's jaws.

9

Although a few species of lizards have a long and forked tongue, similar to that of snakes, most of the North American species have a short, stubby tongue with little bifurcation (division into two branches). Unlike snakes that seem to flick out their tongues almost continually, lizards keep the tongue in the mouth except when they are hunting for food or are engaged in a courtship ritual. Even then, they extend the tongue only occasionally and rather slowly. An exception must be noted in the case of the true chameleon which uses its tongue to capture insects. The chameleon's tongue is an amazing organ and is extended so quickly that one usually gets only a fleeting glimpse of it.

The Nostrils

In the turtles, lizards, and snakes the nostrils are placed close together at the anterior (front) part of the head or snout. In the crocodiles and alligators the openings of the nose are on top of the snout near its tip, a very convenient place for an aquatic animal. The air that enters the nostrils passes above the palate and into the throat, which can be closed by a flap of mucosa. When a crocodile or alligator seizes an animal below the water, the opening of the mouth does not interfere with breathing.

The Eyes

The eyes of turtles are small with a round pupil and an iris which is usually dark in the land forms but often colored in the aquatic species. Turtles' eyes are situated one on each side of the head, and each is guarded by three eyelids: a short, thick, opaque upper lid; a longer, thin lower lid; and a transparent lid (nictitating membrane) that moves over the eyeball from the anterior corner of the eye.

The eyes of snakes vary greatly in size. They are extremely small in some burrowing species and are so large in others that they change the shape of the skull. In most snakes the pupil is round, although it is vertical and catlike in others, and even horizontal in some European forms. The eyes of the blind snakes lie beneath the scales of the head through which they are visible as pigment spots. The eyelids are fused over the eyes, but there is a transparent region which allows them to see. A snake's stare is caused by its inability to close its eyes, that is, to cover them with movable lids. As the eyes are permanently protected by a transparent membrane, snakes can enter the water without the least inconvenience and do not run the risk of getting particles in their eyes. Snakes can sleep with both eyes open. Although they have tear glands, they cannot shed tears the way mammals do.

Except for two species, all North American lizards have functional eyes. Their vision is probably as good as that of many mammals. Several species can detect moving objects at a distance of 100 feet or more. Many lizards have movable eyelids which they close when they are asleep or when they require protection. Others lack movable eyelids but have instead a transparent scale that covers the eyes. These lizards are mostly nocturnal in habit: They nearly all have pupils which, like those of the cat, expand and become round in darkness but contract to vertical slits in bright light. Still others have a moderately large transparent window in the center of the lower lid through which they can see objects even though their eyelids are closed. Experiments have shown that lizards can distinguish color.

The eyes of the crocodiles and alligators are located high on top of the head, which enable the animals to view their surroundings when they are submerged under water.

The Ears

In turtles the tympanic membrane, or eardrum, lies just behind the angle of the jaws. Snakes lack such a structure. A few species of lizards do not show any evidence of external ears and are quite deaf. However, most lizards have external ear openings and can hear reasonably well, though few of them appear to pay much attention to sound. The crocodiles and alligators have well-developed ears which are provided with valves that close when the animals are under water.

Limbs and Locomotion

All turtles have two pairs of limbs, or legs, usually with five fingers and toes that have large horny claws that are useful in crawling, climbing, or digging. The front limbs of some of the completely aquatic species take the form of paddles or flippers. The turtle walks with its limbs sprawled outward at the sides. This gait is very awkward and lumbering. However, a turtle can swim quite easily and rapidly.

Snakes have no limbs. They move by means of lateral (sideways) undulations of the body or by shifting the abdominal scutes forward in alternate sections of the body. To move its body by shifting scutes, the snake presses the rough posterior (rear)

11

edges of the abdominal scutes against its belly, the substratum. Most snakes cannot move forward very well on a smooth surface, however, all species are able to swim. Most snakes can also climb. Certain tree-loving species found in Asia and the Malay Archipelago leap so easily from tree to tree that they are said to fly. Snakes seem to move swiftly over the ground, but this is an optical illusion created by their slender forms.

Most lizards have four limbs or legs; however, a few species lost their limbs during evolution.

We have only to compare the limbs of various species to observe the ways they have become adapted to suit the habitat they occupy. Some lizards have curious parallel ridges on the lower surface of their toes that aid them in getting over the ground; others have adhesive pads at the tips of their digits, or toes, to help them to climb and move on smooth surfaces. Lizards that live on sand dunes have fringes along the toes that enable them to travel on the sand. Even the claws show modifications. In the arboreal, or tree-dwelling, species they are strong and curved.

Lizards are agile creatures. Those with well-developed limbs walk and run without much effort and can move over the ground quickly. When unusual speed is needed, some species rear up on their hind legs in order to run faster. Species with short legs and long bodies are not able to travel over the ground as well as those with well-developed limbs. For short-legged lizards locomotion is more a matter of crawling than walking. Species that have lost their limbs entirely, like the limbless forms, move by means of a series of serpentine or snakelike movements. Lizards are able to hop and most forms can swim though they are not completely aquatic.

Like turtles and lizards, crocodiles and alligators have four large, well-developed legs with five digits on the fore limbs and four webbed digits on the hind limbs. When swimming, they fold their legs against the body. On land the legs can carry them with surprising speed for short distances. When moving on land crocodiles and alligators do not drag themselves about as many people think, but raise their bodies high off the ground.

The Tail

A turtle's tail is short and stubby, a snake's slender and tapering. In snakes, the tail is about a fourth of the total length of the body, but it may be a third or even two-fifths, as in the rough green snake. Some short-tailed colubrid species have tails that are only about an eighth of their total length. A snake's tail may end in an enlarged spine-like scale, and it is probable that some such structure gave rise to the rattle of a rattlesnake. The tail of sea snakes is flattened and oarlike.

The lizards can discard their tails and grow new ones. Some species do so on the slightest provocation, either voluntarily or in response to a slight blow. Others are reluctant to shed their tails and do so only under great stress. The form of the tail varies greatly. It may be extremely short or quite long. Some lizards have tails that are more than three times as long as their head and body. The tail may be the same diameter as the lizard's body or it may differ in diameter. It may have the same scales as the body or have different ones. It usually tapers toward the end.

As the original tail is an extension of the lizard's backbone and therefore has vertebrae, we might expect that when a tail or part of a tail is cast off, it would be broken off between two successive or connecting vertebrae or at the joint connecting two successive vertebrae. But this is not the case. The plane of fracture, or break, is through one of the vertebrae, either at the middle or near one end. The muscles also separate easily, leaving on the animal's stump a series of cone-shaped depressions at which point a new tail is regenerated. It has been shown experimentally that when a lizard's tail is broken between two vertebrae it will not be regenerated.

A new, or regenerated, tail does not contain vertebrae like those in the original tail but consists instead of cartilage that grows from the stump. New muscles also develop to replace those lost. A regenerated tail is rarely as long as the original. The scales on its surface are not arranged the way they were on the original tail. They also lack the pigments that form the scale pattern. A lizard can regrow its tail a number of times. In rare cases a tail may be partly fractured but not actually broken off. When that happens a new tail will develop from the break. The animal also keeps the old tail and now has a forked tail.

Lizards use the tail for grasping, balancing and for the storage of reserve food supplies in the form of fat. This storage function is of considerable value to species that hibernate or remain inactive for long periods of time. Hibernating lizards are less apt to part with their tails, for by doing so they lose the fat stores needed to carry them through periods of fasting.

Most of North American lizards use the tail for balancing,

and this appears to be its most important function. You have only to watch a lizard that has lost its tail run over the ground or try to climb in a bush or tree to realize how important the tail is for balancing. If deprived of their tails, lizards can no longer run on their hind legs for greater speed. Few North American species have a true prehensible or grasping tail. Those that do use the tail for grasping, crudely hook it over a twig or branch to prevent themselves from falling, but that is about the extent of its use.

The tail is a most important part of the bodies of the crocodiles and alligators. Without the tail they would be unable to move through water. The tail is also a powerful defensive weapon. An enraged crocodilian uses it with a swift sideswipe that is powerful enough to knock a man down.

HABITATS

Turtles occur in freshwater ponds and streams, in swamps and woodlands, and in the sea. Snakes are found in a variety of habitats. Snakes appear to be not too particular where they live and they range over various environments. Certain species, however, are limited as to habitat. The banded sand snake and the horned rattlesnake are not found anywhere except in deserts, while the blind snakes live underground like earthworms and do not come to the surface except when forced out by rains or floods. In the tropics there are some species that spend their entire lives in the trees, almost never descending to the ground.

Lizards also live in many different kinds of habitats—woodlands, forests, fields, rocky places, deserts, and sand dunes. One species, the European common lizard, actually occurs within the Arctic Circle in the Scandinavian Peninsula. A few others invade the polar wastes at times. No North American species take to the air. Asian flying dragons, or draco volans, have wings formed by a thin membrane of skin supported by elongated ribs which enables them to volplane, or glide through the air, much like flying squirrels. The United States does not have any species that take to water like the marine iguana of the Galapagos Islands which goes into the sea to feed on seaweed. However, many species do not hesitate to seek refuge in water when they are alarmed or pursued. The Cuban lizard and the large monitors are excellent swimmers. The monitors are sometimes seen swimming in the ocean some distance from land.

Many factors determine where a lizard will live—

temperature, light, moisture, texture of soil, availability of food and shelter, and the animal's own adaptability to a particular habitat. Where conditions are especially favorable, lizards will be found in numbers.

Crocodiles and alligators are in a sense amphibious animals, that is, they live on both land and in water. They are found in places like swamps where both land and water are available. Sunny river banks are a favorite haunt.

HABITS

Food and Feeding

Turtles feed on both plants and animals. Some species live almost exclusively on animals and some are vegetarians. Others eat both animals and plants, while a few even devour carrion. Turtles eat only the tender leaves and stems and delicate blossoms of plants because their jaws are unable to chew the tough fibrous parts. The diet of most species consists of small invertebrates, such as earthworms, snails, slugs, thin-shelled bivalves, crayfish, and insects. Larger turtles will eat fishes and amphibians, and the largest will devour small mammals and birds. Sea turtles prey on various kinds of small marine animals. In short, turtles will eat any animal they can overcome. Turtles can fast for months. When they feed as often as other mammals they may grow very fat. By using its flexible neck, an aquatic turtle can lie on the bottom of ponds and streams and reach in all directions for its food.

Most snakes feed on a variety of animal life. Unlike turtles they do not eat plants. The leaves and grass blades that have been found in their stomachs were swallowed accidentally with their prey. The size of its prey is roughly proportional to the size of the snake. The smaller species feed on insects, spiders, slugs, and other small creatures; the larger on fishes, frogs, birds, and small mammals. The type of food eaten by a particular species is largely determined by the kind of environment in which it lives. Water snakes feed on fishes, frogs, tadpoles, and crayfish; desert snakes eat lizards and small mammals.

Snakes obtain their food by foraging. They can live for months without eating, but when food is abundant their appetites are prodigious. Snakes capture their prey by seizing it in the mouth and swallowing it directly; by holding it down with a coil of the body; by constricting it, and by the injection of venom.

15

Venom is used primarily for this purpose, rather than as a defensive tool. Snakes do not crush their prey but squeeze it so that the heart beat stops and the animal is quickly killed.

Many lizards are insectivorous or insect-eating. They feed on a variety of insects, though many will eat spiders, scorpions, and other' invertebrates. A few lizards (chuckwalla) feed on plants or on parts of plants, and some (leopard lizards) prey on other lizards, small mammals, bird hatchlings, and bird eggs.

Both crocodiles and alligators are carnivorous, or meat eating, animals. They eat all kinds of animals from insects to large mammals and at times will also eat carrion. Normally they kill their prey and devour it at once, though they have been known to bury food, presumably to ripen it. Because crocodiles and alligators are able to see above water while submerged, they can capture animals floating on the surface or seize those that come to drink at the water's edge.

Courtship

In turtles courtship involves only the pursuit of the female by the male, though it may sometimes take the form of harmlessly biting and pushing her as well. Some of the giant tortoises pound their mates violently. The male tortoises use their bodies like battering rams and at the same time utter loud roars. The male painted turtle gently strokes the face of the female with his long fingernails as he swims in front of her.

Little is known about the courtship of snakes. The male garter and water snake rubs his chin along the back of the female until he reaches the neck region, while the female remains passive. The males have minute sensory organs in the chin, and rubbing against the female serves to stimulate them. The racers engage in a sort of courtship dance in which both sexes take part.

Once a male lizard has located a female responsive to his advances he proceeds to court her by nudging and nipping her. He frequently postures or struts about to display some brilliantly colored part of his body and also bobs his head. Following this performance, he grasps her by the neck and mating takes place.

Courtship in the crocodilians consists of bellowing and roaring by the male, together with characteristic posturing in which the neck is arched and the tail waved from side to side. After this display the male lunges for the female and seizes her by the back of the neck with his jaws.

Mating

Aquatic turtles mate in the water; land species do so either on land or in water. During the mating act, the male mounts the female and usually grasps the front of her shell with his claws. He may come in contact with her posteriorly by merely placing his limbs beneath her shell. During the mating process the male frequently utters a sound. Snakes usually mate in the spring after they emerge from hibernation and before they have scattered for the summer. Mating may also occur during the summer.

In the lizards and crocodilians, mating follows seizure of the female by the male.

Egg-laying

Female turtles lay their eggs in a flask-shaped cavity that they have excavated in the ground. The depth of these cavities, or nests, is determined by the length of the female's hind legs. In a few cases, the fore legs may be employed first to make a shallow basin in the center of which the cavity is then dug. The care exercised in egg-laying varies. Some mud turtles drop single eggs in shallow holes and even leave them half buried; sea turtles bury their eggs in the sand of the beach and then remove all signs that show where they are laid.

Snakes lay their eggs in a variety of places—decaying vegetation, leaf mold, rotting logs, manure piles, sawdust or other debris from a lumberyard, or in holes in various places such as embankments, old walls, decaying roots, and animal burrows. In some species, like the ring-necked snakes, a number of females may lay their eggs at the same site. The king cobra builds a true nest. Although it looks like a heap of leaves, it has two compartments: one below for the eggs, the other above and separate for the guarding parent.

Although a few lizards give birth to living young, most lay eggs. The eggs are laid soon after mating, usually in a hole excavated by the female in a location that is somewhat moist and protected from the direct rays of the sun. Lizards do not build true nests, although in a few species, such as the western skink, there is a slight attempt to build a nest and to brood over the eggs.

The female American alligator, builds a sizable nest in which to lay her eggs. The nest is made of a variety of vegetable trash—leaves, leaf litter, roots, stalks, and stems—all scraped together in a large mound six or eleven feet in diameter and two to three feet high. A female may use the same nest year after year, simply adding a little more material to the top each year. Once the mound is built, she scoops out a hole in the top and lays her eggs inside the mound. After she has laid the eggs, she covers them with some of the nest material and packs it down. Sometimes she puts mud on top and she often crawls back and forth over the top to complete the incubator. The female American crocodile, unlike the American alligator, does not build up a large mound of vegetation but is satisfied to bury her eggs in a large, low mound of sand where the heat of the sun incubates them.

The Eggs

Female turtles normally lay only one clutch of eggs a year, though the green turtle may lay as many as seven in a single season. The number of eggs in a clutch ranges from one in Tornier's tortoise to at least 200 in some sea turtles. The common snapping turtle may lay as many as eighty, more than twice the number of an average clutch. Most turtle eggs are elliptical in shape, but some are spherical, or nearly so. Those of the snapping turtle are surprisingly like ping-pong balls, although somewhat smaller, and they even bounce well. Turtle eggs are not colored. Color would serve no useful purpose in eggs that are always buried. The shell is either flexible or brittle.

All snake eggs are circular in one cross-section, oval in the other. The more slender species may lay eggs with one diameter three to four times as great as the other. Snake eggs are white or cream colored. As they are always concealed the eggs do not need a protectively colored shell as do those of birds. Snake eggs have a tough, parchment-like shell formed of layers of minute fibers. The fibers of one layer lie at right angles to those of the next and are laid down as the eggs pass through the oviducts of the female. At the same time calcium carbonate is deposited, giving the eggs a granular appearance.

The size of snake eggs varies roughly with the size of the snakes that lay them. The average egg of the Indian python measures four and three quarters inches in its greater diameter which is about twice that of the lesser. A blind snake with a body diameter of only an eighth of an inch lays a very small egg which is rather elongated. Some small snakes lay eggs that are rather large. The eggs of the little smooth green snake measure one inch in length; those of the bull snake are little more than two inches long. Snakes normally lay their eggs during June and July and even into early August. In some species the eggs adhere tightly to one another; in others they are free.

Not all snakes lay eggs. Some give birth to living young. These snakes produce their young from late July to early October. Until recently it was believed that live-bearing snakes retained the eggs in the oviducts. But it is now known that in some snakes the embryos are nourished by the mother somewhat as they are in mammals. The number of young in a brood varies greatly, even among individuals of the same species. As a rule small snakes have fewer young than large ones. Garter and water snakes are very prolific. There are records of a garter snake having as many as seventy-eight young and a water snake seventy-six. The average number of young produced is about ten or less, and some species do not have more than three or four.

Lizard eggs vary in number from one to about twenty-five, depending on the species. They are white or nearly so when laid but soon become stained and lose their whiteness. The eggs usually hatch in late summer or early fall in time for the hatchlings to reach a moderate size before going into hibernation.

The American alligator lays from fifteen to eighty-eight hard, brittle, oblong eggs from May to July.

Incubation of Eggs

The incubation of turtle eggs takes two or three months depending on temperature and humidity. It is not uncommon for eggs and hatchlings to live through the winter in northern regions. The incubation period of snakes depends on the state of development of the embryo at the time of laying and on the temperature at which the eggs are kept. There is no definite period of incubation for any of the species. Eggs have been known to hatch within four days after they were laid, whereas some have required more than three months to hatch. As a rule hatching occurs during August and September. Young snakes are able to fend for themselves from the moment they enter the world.

The incubation period in lizards varies according to the species. In the green anole it is six to seven weeks; in the northern fence lizard eight to ten weeks; in the Texas horned lizard five to nine weeks; in the six-lined race runner five to eight weeks; in the western collared lizard nine to ten weeks; and in the western skink five to six weeks.

The incubation period in the American alligator is nine to ten weeks.

Fig. 6   Hatchling snapping turtle

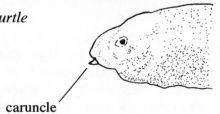

caruncle

Hatching of Reptile Eggs

It is rather difficult for the young turtle, snake, or lizard to rupture its egg shell. Both embryonic turtles and crocodilians are provided with a horny caruncle on the tip of the snout to help them make a hole in the shell. (Fig. 6) Embryonic lizards and snakes have an egg tooth that protrudes from the front of the roof of the mouth. (Fig. 7) The egg tooth is a true tooth carried on the maxillary bone and is quite different from the caruncle of the turtles and crocodilians. The egg tooth is shed a short time after the young hatch. In the geckos, the embryonic lizards have a pair of egg teeth instead of a single tooth and in this respect they differ from all other lizards. The red-eared turtle carries the caruncle for about ten days, the box turtles for two or three weeks and the snapping turtles for three to four weeks.

When the embryo reaches the end of the incubation period, the caruncle or egg tooth is well developed and the embryo has grown to the point where it presses against the egg shell. A single large tear or cut in the shell may be sufficient to permit the hatchling to emerge, but sometimes additional openings are needed. Some lizards and some turtles use the sharp claws of the feet to rip open the shell or to enlarge the original break made by the egg tooth or caruncle. Meanwhile, as the time of hatching approaches, the inner part of the egg shell is eroded away by enzyme action so that the shell becomes very thin, especially near the head of the embryo. The thinning process makes hatching much easier, but there are occasions when an individual hatchling is unable to escape from the egg.

Fig. 7   Milk snake

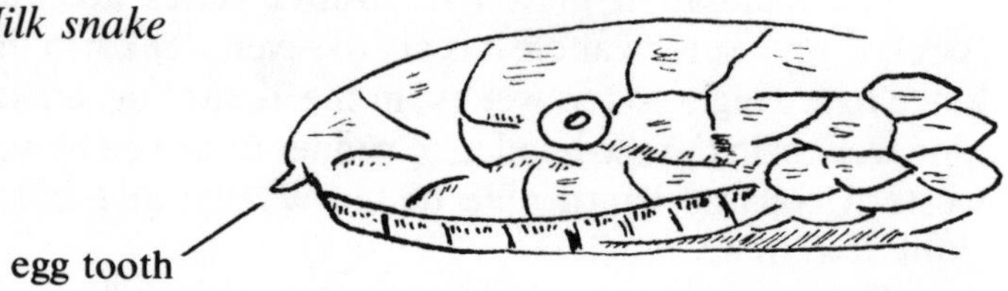

egg tooth

20

Parental Care

No parental care is exercised by the turtles. Once the eggs have been laid the females show no further interest in them. Snakes guard their eggs, though the live-bearing species show no interest in their young. The females of many egg-layers remain coiled about their eggs and, in some instances, defend them vigorously when beset by an intruder. There is some evidence that the Indian and king cobras pair during the breeding season and take turns guarding their eggs. On the whole, snakes show little concern either for their eggs or their young. This may be because the hatchlings, or new-born young, are able to care for themselves and can even live as long as a year without any food at all.

Parental care is unknown among the lizards.

During the period of incubation, the female American alligator has been reported to wet its nest material several times by emptying the contents of her bladder on the mound. She also remains in the vicinity of the nest, usually in an adjacent hole, or in some similar spot, until she hears the high-pitched grunting sounds that the young make on hatching. If the nest is packed too hard for the young to get out by themselves, the female scrapes away the top of the nest to free them. Once they are out of the nest she often shepherds them around for from one to three years. She also excavates a wallow pool or cove from ten to twenty feet in diameter for the young and remains nearby to to protect them from predators.

Sunning

Water turtles have the habit of coming out of the water onto a projecting rock or floating log to bask in the sun. Land turtles also sun themselves but not to the same extent. Sunning probably regulates an animal's body temperature, helps to rid it of leeches and other external parasites and to slow down the growth of algae. Sunning has its disadvantages because it advertises the presence and whereabouts of the turtles to any predator that might be in the vicinity. Snakes usually lie in the sun for a while before going into hibernation and also upon emerging from it.

Hibernation

As turtles and snakes cannot withstand low temperatures, they spend the winter in some warm retreat, in other words, they hibernate. Hibernation occurs when the temperature falls toward the freezing point, but they become slightly sluggish when it is a little under 60 degrees F. Aquatic species, such as the painted and spotted turtles, dig into the bottom mud of ponds and streams and remain there until the temperature rises in the spring. Wood turtles that wander over the pastures in the summer also hibernate under water. Box turtles and other land forms remain on land and bury themselves in dry, as well as moist, soil.

Except for species that live in the South, most North American snakes are dormant in the winter. In autumn they begin to gather on southern slopes and sun-warmed ledges. There they lie in the sun near one another or with their bodies intertwined, seeming to postpone their long sleep as much as possible. Eventually they go into winter quarters which may be an animal burrow, a cavity beneath a boulder, or in an old stone wall, or in a deep hole in a bank or in one left by a decaying root. Many snakes may enter the same retreat, or it may be occupied by only a single snake. The most striking winter behavior of snakes is their habit of forming hibernating balls, which are clusters of intertwined snakes that vary from two or three to hundreds. They are similar to the balls in which earthworms spend the winter or dry spells in summer. These balls help to conserve moisture and prevent the body temperature from falling too low.

Turtles and snakes cannot withstand low temperatures because they are cold-blooded. Lizards, too, must find some place where they can safely pass the winter. A lizard's winter refuge may be under loose bark, in rotting logs or stumps, under rocks, beneath leaf cover, or in the ground. The depths the animals burrow into the ground depends on the species, the texture of the soil, temperature, and the animal's age. Young lizards hibernate at more shallow depths than the adults. How long a lizard will hibernate and to what extent it may become dormant is determined by the resistance of the species and the weather. A lizard living in northern regions will remain in hibernation longer than one in southern. Some southern lizards do not hibernate but hide in a secluded place when the temperature gets low and reappear when it becomes warm again.

Methods of Defense

The turtle's shell appears to be an adequate defense against all predatory animals except humans. Hatching turtles, however, do not have a hard shell and are vulnerable to many flesh-eating animals. Many species of turtles practice active methods of self-protection. Very young turtles are often masters in the art of concealment. The soft-shelled are astonishingly swift in flight and may claw and bite viciously when seized. Snapping turtles can be most formidable. Some turtles have glands that give off unpleasant odors that seem to be protective. In musk and mud turtles the substances causing these odors are secreted by four glands that open directly to the exterior at the edges of the shell.

Most animals when threatened with danger seek escape in flight and snakes are no exception. However, rattlesnakes often stop and assume a defensive coil; their large size, heavy bodies, and slow movements make flight difficult. Like most animals when cornered or seized, snakes will strenuously defend themselves in a variety of ways, though biting is the usual defense. Biting is most effective in species with a poison apparatus. The vast majority of snakes do not have this lethal weapon. In all the harmless snakes, the teeth are numerous and needle-sharp but produce only a group of tiny punctures. These punctures often bleed profusely because the snake's saliva retards or prevents the coagulation of the victim's blood, and the wound looks worse than it really is.

When seized some species of snakes pour out a secretion from the anal scent glands. The secretion has a penetrating musky or sweetish odor and usually causes the would-be predator to release its intended victim. Other snakes rear up and strike when confronted with danger. Pine snakes and bull snakes accompany each strike by a hiss which sounds like escaping steam and can be most frightening. Still other snakes flatten their bodies on the ground to make them appear much larger, while other snakes do quite the reverse and inflate their bodies until their look like toy balloons. The rubber boa, when annoyed, often rolls itself into a compact ball with its head in the center; blue racers, whip snakes, and even garter snakes sometimes use this trick. Probably the most remarkable defensive behavior is the extraordinary death feint of the hog-nosed snake, which is described in Chapter 18.

Lizards have many ways of defending themselves against their enemies. Terrestrial, or ground-dwelling, species flee from predators, though flight is not always effective. Even the fastest lizards are sometimes overtaken before they reach a refuge. The arboreal, or tree-dwelling, species also run for a distance before they seek safety by climbing trees and bushes where they are lost to sight. Both forms may also freeze and try to escape notice by becoming inconspicuous.

Some species inflate their bodies when captured to make themselves more difficult to swallow. The horned lizards, whose horns are a particularly successful protective device, inflate their bodies most effectively. Horned lizards can also eject a stream of blood to help defend themselves.

Many species will bite viciously if attacked or cornered, others will scratch, but only the large species have claws big enough to be effective. A few lash their tails around like a whip. If the tails have spines they can cause a great deal of damage to an attacker. A number of species open their mouths and hiss or squeak feebly; such behavior is probably of some defensive value.

A great many lizards are protectively colored and escape detection by blending into their surroundings. Lizards that have been captured often play possum. By feigning death, they trick their enemies into letting them go, then suddenly they return to life and dart away to safety.

Undoubtedly the most interesting of all lizard defensive measures is that of casting off the tail. When severed from the body, the tail bounds, bounces and wriggles so vigorously that the predator's attention is distracted from the lizard itself. As the predator watches the tail, the fleeing lizard slinks away and grows a new tail.

Both crocodiles and alligators are amply protected by their armor-like covering, powerful tail and jaws and hence have few if any enemies, except human beings.

Bobbing

Some lizards have the peculiar habit of bobbing or moving the body up and down. We don't know the reason for this unusual behavior, but it is probably a form of nervous behavior associated with alertness.

Growth

Turtles achieve most of their growth during their first year. Growth does not stop then but continues at a much reduced rate for an undetermined period of time. Most species reach maturity in three to seven years. Snakes differ from other animals in that they do not stop growing when they become mature. Their rate of growth merely slows down though they continue to grow at a gradually diminishing rate as long as they live. The red-bellied snake becomes sexually mature during the second year, the rattlesnake during the third.

We do not know how fast lizards grow. Their growth appears to stop during the first hibernating period of the newly hatched young, then resumes in their second year. By their third year most lizards have reached their adult size. Thereafter they grow very slowly.

We also do not know how fast most crocodilians grow. Probably the usual rate of growth is about ten to twelve inches a year. In its natural habitat the American alligator grows rapidly. At two years it is about forty inches; at four years, sixty-two; and at six years, seventy-two.

SENSES AND INTELLIGENCE

The sense of hearing in turtles is not well developed. But turtles respond so readily to vibrations through the skin that they are easily frightened by a noise of any kind. Their sense of smell appears to be fairly acute at close range, and they are able to distinguish between various kinds of food both in and out of water. The skin over many parts of the turtle's body is very sensitive to touch. They are able to see rather well, and certain species can distinguish one color from another. Most surprising is the turtle's ability to learn. Certain species, such as the painted turtle, have been able to learn to discriminate between patterns of vertical and horizontal black and white lines. The wood turtle is about equal to a rat in learning to go through a maze.

Snakes have no external eardrum so in that sense they can be said to be totally deaf. However, the inner ear is well developed and doubtless sounds carried through the ground are heard well enough. The sense of sight and smell are well developed. Their vision is very acute though they can probably see only for short distances. Smell is very important. It helps snakes to follow their prey and to recognize other members of their own kind, as well as the sex of various individuals.

The most important sensory organ in snakes is the tongue, which is not a stinger, but a very sensitive organ of touch. When a snake flicks its tongue in and out of its mouth the fine tips are touched lightly to the ground, informing the snake about the nature of the ground over which it is moving. The tongue is also an aid in smelling. The delicate tips pick up minute particles and transfer them to tiny cavities in the front of the roof of the mouth.

These cavities, or pits, which are lined with delicate sensory cells, are known as Jacobson's organ and are an adaptation of the smelling area of the nose. Snakes apparently have no sense of taste. This is not surprising. Taste would be of little value to animals that swallow their prey whole and without chewing. The facial pits that are situated on either side of the face in rattlesnakes and their relatives is a special sense organ used to detect delicate heat waves. Experiments have shown that they help these snakes to direct their strike.

Many lizards can hear well. In a few species, such as the geckos, voice plays an important role in their social life. However, most species do not appear to pay much attention to sound. Except for two species, all North American lizards have functional eyes, and their vision is probably as good as that of many mammals. Several species can detect moving objects at a distance of 100 feet or more. Many lizards have movable eyelids which they can close when they are asleep or when they require protection. Others lack movable eyelids but have instead a transparent scale that covers the eye. These lizards are mostly nocturnal in habit. They nearly all have pupils which, like those of the cat, expand and become round in the darkness but contract to mere vertical slits in bright light. Still other lizards have a moderately large transparent window in the center of the lower lid through which they can see objects even though their eyelids are closed. Lizards can distinguish color. Many have a parietal eye, sometimes called a third eye, located in the top center of the head behind the eyes. The parietal eye does not function as an eye in the sense of providing an image, but serves as a light receptor to detect the presense or direction of light. Like snakes, lizards also have a Jacobson's organ.

Both crocodiles and alligators have well developed ears and fairly good vision. Voice plays an important part in the alligator's territorial organization and in reproduction.

TERRITORY

Following the emergence from hibernation in the spring (the time varies with the species and with the locality), adult lizards feed for a week or two and then engage in courtship and mating which may last for several days. At this time the males stake out a territory. They defend this area against other males of the same species that may attempt to encroach upon their domain. They

26

engage in sham fights, puffing up, and displaying their bright colors to fullest advantage in an effort to intimidate the intruder and frighten him away. Failing this, they attack him violently, desisting only when he has been driven beyond the limits of their territory.

Both male and female alligators maintain a fairly definite territory. The bellowing of the males serves the double purpose of keeping away intruding males and of attracting the females. Should the bellowing fail to win a mate, the male may resort to fighting; the females will fight to keep other females and small males from encroaching on their territory.

SEX DIFFERENCES

As a rule the female turtle is larger than the male. Sometimes she is twice as large as the male or has three times his bulk. Among the soft-shelled turtles the female may attain two or three times the bulk of the male. In a few species the old males have relatively large heads, in others it is the females. Sometimes the belly of the male is noticeably concave, while that of the female is flat. Differences in color are rare. The most noticeable mark of the male is his long tail. In snakes the male and female are usually so much alike that it is difficult to distinguish between them.

In many species of lizards, there are no external features to distinguish the sexes, but in others there are marked differences. The male fence lizard is smaller than the female. The male collared lizard has an enlarged head, caused by its highly developed jaw muscles, which it uses to grip the female in mating; it is more brightly colored than the female. The male green anole has a throat fan, or dewlap, while the male striped ground uta sometimes has a different color pattern from that of the female.

ECONOMIC IMPORTANCE OF REPTILES

People have been eating turtles since prehistoric times. Sea turtles have provided a constant source of food. These large reptiles are found throughout the world and are easy to capture when they come ashore to lay their eggs. In the United States the turtles of commercial value are the diamond-back terrapin of the brackish waters of the east coast and the alligator and common snapping turtles. The soft-shelled turtles are relished in the United States, and all over the world, especially in China and

27

Japan. The eggs of the sea turtles are everywhere considered a delicacy.

Turtle shells are used in the arts and crafts. The shell of the hawksbill is the source of tortoise shell. The Romans valued tortoise shell as a veneer for furniture, but in modern times it has been used mainly in the making of toilet articles, ornamental buhl furniture, and as a veneer for small boxes and frames. A high grade oil is extracted from turtle fat. Some turtles are of value in destroying harmful insects and other invertebrates. Snapping turtles are useful scavengers.

Some of the larger species of snakes help to keep down the number of mice and rats in grain and hay fields. A few snakes are eaten as food. The eastern diamondback rattlesnake is sold in cans in an a la king preparation. The skins of rattlesnakes are often tanned for use as belts, pocketbooks, wallets, ties, shoes, and other small items. Snake venoms are used in the manufacture of counteragents (antivenoms) for the treatment of snakebite and for other purposes.

Lizards are essentially insectivorous, or insect-eating, and are useful in keeping harmful insects in check. In some parts of the country they help to control insects destructive to various crops, such as grasshoppers, the beet leafhopper, and the chinch bug. Lizards themselves serve as food for other animals, particularly snakes and birds. Although all lizards can presumably be eaten by human beings, only the chuckwalla is eaten in the United States and only to a very limited extent. Some tropical species, such as the monitors, are valuable for their skins which are converted into leather for shoes and other articles.

The hides of the crocodilians provide excellent leather for use in the manufacture of shoes, trunks, travelling bags, pocketbooks, and various novelties. At one time alligators were eaten in large numbers by the Seminole Indians and the natives of the southern states. In recent years the exploitation of both crocodiles and alligators has declined because laws now regulate the hunting of these animals.

REPTILES AS SUBJECTS FOR STUDY

Keeping reptiles as pets can be a lot of fun, but it is more interesting and meaningful if you try to learn as much as you can about them. We know a great deal about some of our native species but very little about others. With careful observation it is

28

possible that you may add to our knowledge. This would be a source of great satisfaction and a real accomplishment.

Any study is of little value unless you keep an accurate record of all your observations. Record them in a notebook at the time you make them, or immediately afterward, because if you wait you may forget what you saw. Be very careful to interpret your observations as correctly or accurately as possible. It is important to keep a record of individual specimens and not of a whole group if you have several of the same species.

You might record how often a certain turtle, lizard, or snake eats, and what and how much it eats. When it is active, when it rests, and how it sleeps. How quickly it grows, and what its increase is in weight and size. How long it remains in the open and how long under cover. How often it sheds its skin. No doubt other observations will come to mind.

If you study captive reptiles, at some time you may want to study them in their natural surroundings. Such a study is most important, as the habits and behavior of animals in the wild are more normal than those of the species in captivity. And both studies complement each other.

How, When, and Where to Obtain Reptiles

There are two ways to obtain reptiles for pets: go where they occur and capture them or buy them at a pet store or from a reptile dealer. (A list of dealers is given in the appendix.)

All the reptiles described in this book are small, harmless, that is, nonpoisonous, though some may bite, species that can usually be picked up by hand. Those that are commonly found under rocks, logs and similar cover can be collected by quickly overturning the cover and then quickly seizing the animals before they get away. Species that take refuge in mammal holes, in crevices, in rocks, and in similar places can be followed, then dug out, using a trowel or shovel. Lizards that you cannot approach closely enough to seize with the hand can often be caught with a noose at the end of a thread, two or three feet long, dangling from a stick, three or four feet long. If you approach a lizard with such a device, the animal will focus its attention on you and be unaware of the noose until it has been slipped around its body. Lizards may also be caught by stunning them momentarily with a blow from a slender twig, or by hitting them with a handful of earth.

Snakes, like garter snakes, can be captured by gently step-

ping on them and then picking them up, or you can pin them
down with the aid of a snake stick, which is an L-shaped instru-
ment consisting of a long stick with an angle iron at one end.
(Fig. 8.)

It is best to put the captive reptiles in cloth bags or in bags
made from heavy, sturdy plastic, using a separate bag for each
specimen. Place the animals in their permanent quarters as soon
as possible.

You might try collecting lizards at night. With the aid of a
flashlight the animals may be discovered as they sleep, or when
aroused from their hiding place.

If you live in the South, where reptiles are active throughout
the year, you can collect them all year, but in the North, where
they hibernate during the winter, they may be secured only
during the warmer months.

As some wild animals may be protected in some states and
provinces and not in others, it is advisable to check with the local
wildlife department or write to the Fish and Wildlife Service

Fig. 8   Snake stick

——— angle iron

District Law Enforcement Office nearest your home before you
go out and capture a turtle, lizard, or snake, or buy one from a pet
store or reptile dealer. (The addresses of these offices are listed in
the Appendix.)

Aquatic turtles are no longer sold in pet stores unless their
shells measure more than four inches in diameter. The sale of
small turtles has been outlawed because they carry several kinds
of bacteria belonging to the genus salmonella which can be
transmitted to humans and other animals. The bacteria is the
source of a type of food poisoning known as *salmonellosis*.

Some species of reptiles, when newly captured, will make
no effort to escape, and you will have no trouble in handling
them. Others, however, will make every attempt to free themselves, and with these you will have to use force to prevent them
from escaping. Use as little force as necessary and be very careful
not to injure the animals. Never pick up a lizard by the tail, but
always by the body. Never squeeze a lizard's neck, as this will
only make the animal struggle more vigorously.

Though some reptiles adjust to captivity, they do not adjust

31

to being handled and therefore should not be picked up unless there is a good reason for doing so. Do not handle any of your pets more than is necessary. When you must handle them, be as gentle as you can and avoid any quick or sudden movements.

If the time should ever come when you do not want to keep your reptile pets any longer, or for some reason cannot do so, do not let them go just anyplace. Release them where you found them originally. If this is not possible, give them to a zoo, or museum, or to some organization equipped to care for them, otherwise you doom your pets to a slow death and disturb a delicately balanced ecosystem.

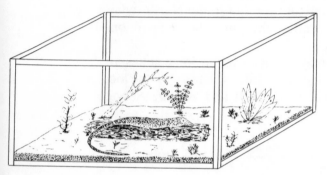

Fig. 9   Woodland terrarium

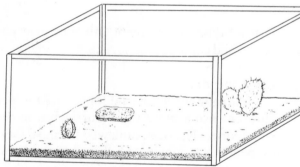

Fig. 10   Desert terrarium

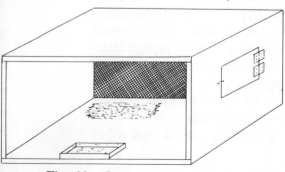

Fig. 11   Cage

The Care of Reptile Pets

HOUSING

To keep reptile pets successfully it is essential that they be contented and healthy. They must be provided with living quarters that imitate their natural surroundings as closely as possible.

A fish tank or tropical fish aquarium is the best kind of quarters. Be sure to get one large enough. It should be at least fifteen inches in length and eight to ten inches in width and depth. Such an aquarium can easily be converted into a woodland terrarium (Fig. 9), a desert terrarium (Fig. 10), or a semi-aquatic habitat (a terrarium divided into two sections by a glass partition. The "swimming" section is filled with water, and the land section is filled with equal amounts of sand and humus, small rocks, plants, and twigs. A small log slope, or ramp, permits the reptile to easily climb out of the water onto the land portion). There are other advantages to using an aquarium: the glass sides permit clear vision; drafts of cold air, which are detrimental to desert species are excluded; and, equally important, temperature and humidity can be more easily controlled. Be sure to keep the top covered with some sort of screening to prevent your pets from escaping. A frame of wood to which a piece of wire screening is attached will do nicely.

If you find an aquarium too expensive and are adept with tools, you can make one by setting four panes of glass in a wood frame with a galvanized metal bottom (over solid wood) on which a dish pan is fitted. A serviceable cage can be made from a wooden box. Remove two opposite sides and replace one by wire screening and the other by glass (Fig. 11). You can also make a cage of wire screening with a wood base and frame. But in any case the cage must have a hinged door so that you can have access to the animals in order to feed them and to clean the cage.

The word terrarium is used for a cage or container in which land animals and plants are kept and which simulates their natural surroundings as much as possible. Woodland species require a woodland terrarium. Place one or two inches of sand or gravel on the bottom of an aquarium or fish tank. This will provide drainage from the upper layer of soil which must be moistened from time to time. Add a layer of woods loam or good soil to a depth of about one and a half inches. Spread the soil evenly over the bottom layer of sand or gravel. Next add some ferns, mosses, liverworts, perhaps a pine seedling or two, or some other low-growing plants. To make the woodland terrarium seem even more natural, place one or two-lichen-covered stones on top of the soil as well as a piece of wood covered with fungus. Because some species of reptiles burrow or dig and are likely to uproot the plants, root them in flowerpots. Place the flowerpots in the terrarium with the bottom of each flowerpot resting on the sand or gravel layer. Depending on the kind of animals that will inhabit the terrarium it might be best in some cases to use hothouse plants instead of those that grow in the wild, in other words, plants that will stand watering every day.

For desert dwelling species, prepare a desert terrarium by placing a layer of clean sand several inches deep in the aquarium, adding some small stones or rocks, a small log or pieces of bark. A few small cactus plants might also be included. The cacti should be placed in the sand in flowerpots to prevent them from being uprooted when the animals burrow.

For animals like turtles that live in water but spend some time on land, or that like to bask in the sun on a projecting rock or floating log, provide a semi-aquatic terrarium. This is an environment that is part terrarium and part aquarium. A semi-aquatic terrarium can be made by placing a partition across the aquarium and filling one half with soil or pebbles and the other half with water. The partition can be made of slate or some similar material (it can even be a piece of wood) that is held in place by inserting small wooden wedges between the partition and the glass sides of the aquarium. Depending on the size of the turtles, make a ramp with a small stone or a piece of bark. The soil or pebble part, the beach, in other words, might have a small potted plant or two and a shelter of some kind. Instead of building a semi-aquatic terrarium you might prefer merely to sink a photo-developing tray or a similar dish in a woodland terrarium. The tray or dish serves as a pond or pool.

If you have a backyard, wood and box turtles may be kept outdoors in an enclosure made of chicken wire. The enclosure might measure five feet by eight feet, or if it is to be circular, five feet in diameter. Insert the wire into the ground to a depth of several inches to keep the turtles from escaping by burrowing beneath it. The top of the wire should have an overhang so that the turtles cannot escape by climbing over it. Build a shallow pool of stone or concrete with a drain if possible to let out the dirty water. In the summertime it may be necessary to clean out the pool almost every day. The wire should not be so high that you cannot step over it easily. If possible a shady spot should be selected for the enclosure, which should be provided with one or two shelters. During the winter, box and wood turtles can be taken indoors and kept in a wooden box in a heated room. The box should be sufficiently large so that the animals can move around comfortably.

TEMPERATURE AND LIGHT REQUIREMENTS

Temperature and light are important ecological factors. As both temperature and light fluctuate in their natural surroundings, it is essential that captive animals must be provided with similar variations. They must be given a choice of different temperatures and different amounts of light so that they may thrive and remain healthy. It is also rather apparent that species differ in the degree of variation required or that which they can tolerate.

Proper heat and light can be provided in several ways. The cheapest source of both heat and light is sunlight, which is essential for most lizards. The woodland and semi-aquatic terraria and their inhabitants need to be exposed to sunlight only for an hour or two each day. Then they should be kept in a subdued light which can be achieved by stretching a linen curtain across the window. In a room with direct sunlight, place only a part of the terrarium or cage in its rays and leave part in the shade. Lizards and turtles require some sunshine, but snakes can do without it if they eat well and are given sufficient good food. Lizards are able to stand a certain amount of heat but die if kept in high temperatures. A rectangular all-glass terrarium should never be placed in direct sunlight. The glass concentrates the rays of the sun with disastrous results. A cage made of wire screening may be placed in sunlight for a short time if only part of the cage is exposed and the rest kept in the shade.

The ideal temperature for most reptiles is from 70 to 85 degrees Fahrenheit. Though the cheapest source of heat is sunlight, it is not the most satisfactory because the temperature can not be adequately controlled and may drop too much during the night. The best and safest means of controlling the temperature for reptile pets is an ordinary electric light bulb. By using bulbs of different sizes, both temperature and light can easily be regulated. The bulb, or bulbs, should be placed at one end of the terrarium or cage, with the shelter area at the other end so that the inhabitants can move either directly beneath the heat source or away from it according to need. The size and strength of the bulb can be determined by a little experimentation. The size of the terrarium or cage and the kind of reptile kept in it will also determine the size of the bulb required. For most species a bulb of 60 or 70 watts will be adequate though some desert species may require a bulb of 100 watts or 120 watts. Keep a thermometer in the terrarium or cage at all times and check the temperature regularly.

For species that do not require too much light, an electric heating unit might be used instead of an electric light bulb. The unit should be placed so that the animals cannot come in contact with it, and moreover it should be placed where it will not heat the entire terrarium or cage. Care should be exercised in using electric heating units because too much heat will burn or dry out the animals.

Desert species seem to benefit by the use of an ultraviolet lamp. Ultraviolet light can be supplied by incandescent sunlamps available in most drug and hardware stores. Usually the animals are exposed to the sunlamp for five to twenty minutes a day at a distance of about two feet. Some species appear to eat better when exposed to small amounts of ultraviolet light.

One final word regarding temperature: do not place the

terrarium or cage in a bedroom where the window is opened at night.

MOISTURE AND DRINKING WATER

The amount of moisture necessary for the welfare of reptile pets can be obtained by proper ventilation of the terrarium or cage, by the use of plants, and by regulating the amount of heat supplied. Lizards that live on the desert obtain water from the food they eat. Non-desert species lap up droplets of dew or rainwater from the foliage of plants. Such water can be supplied by sprinkling the terrarium plants, pieces of bark, or other objects with a bulb atomizer. Provide a dish of water for snakes. In a semi-aquatic terrarium the miniature pond or pool will supply the necessary moisture, though the plants should be sprinkled each day.

FOOD AND FEEDING

Aquatic turtles, such as the painted turtle and the spotted turtle, may be fed chopped raw meat, chopped raw fish, earthworms, and soft-bodied insect larvae, as well as canned dog food. Terrestrial species, such as the box and wood turtles, may be given the same diet, as well as lettuce, pieces of banana, sliced carrots, sliced tomatoes, and berries of various kinds.

Although some species of lizards feed on plants and one, the Gila monster, on eggs, they are generally insectivorous. They live on a variety of insects though many lizards will also eat spiders, scorpions, and other invertebrate forms; a few even eat mammals. During the warmer months of the year, one or two sweeps with an insect net through the grass or other vegetation will provide enough insects for at least a single feeding. A piece of fruit placed in the cage or terrarium will attract flies, which some species will take readily. The herbivorous species will eat the plants mentioned in the chapters dealing with these lizards, but with a little experimentation you may find others that they will eat also. Snakes have specialized food habits, but the species mentioned in this book feed largely on insects, snails, slugs, earthworms, and the like. Many snakes feed on mice and rats, frogs, toads, and various small mammals. Such food is rather difficult to obtain, and moreover, it is not desirable to bring such animals into the home. Therefore, we are concerned with only

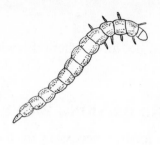

Fig. 12   Mealworm

those snakes that feed on food easily obtainable, and to which your parents can hardly object. Turtles may be fed two or three times a week, lizards every other day, and snakes once a week, or more often if necessary.

Newly obtained specimens may be reluctant to eat, and in that event you will have to exercise a little patience and perhaps some ingenuity. You may also have to spend a little time with your pets until they become accustomed to their new surroundings. If you give them the proper attention in the beginning, you will be surprised at how quickly they will learn to take food. A regular schedule of feeding is important.

Feeding your reptile pets during the summer is a relatively easy matter when insects and earthworms are readily available. But if you live in the North, or in a place where their natural food can not easily be obtained, feeding your pets in the winter will be a problem unless you lay in a supply of such items as mealworms and other foods or can obtain them from a neighborhood pet dealer. To be assured of an adequate supply of food it is advisable to culture mealworms, earthworms, cockroaches, and so on. Directions for doing so follow. The quantity that you require will depend on how many and what kinds of pets you have.

Culturing Mealworms

Mealworms are the larvae of a black beetle known scientifically as *tenebrio molitor* and are easily cultured. The size of the culture depends on how many reptile pets you need to feed. You can use either a tight box, earthen jar, crock, or glass jar. The top should be covered with wire screening. Fill the container half full of food material—breakfast bran, cornmeal, or wheat in some form. Wheat is generally considered to be the best. Add a few bread crusts, a carrot, or half an apple or raw potato, a sheet of crushed newspaper, or a few scraps of old leather, and finally a supply of mealworms, which you can purchase at a pet store or from an animal supply dealer. Place the container in a warm place. The best temperature for growing mealworms is 80 degrees Fahrenheit.

Except for having to replace the bread, carrot, apple, or potato, which supply the moisture for the mealworms, no further care is necessary. When they become full grown, the mealworms pupate. Shortly after the adult beetles appear they will mate and the females will lay several thousand eggs and die. The eggs will hatch into young mealworms which will grow rapidly under the proper conditions. After they have mated and laid their eggs, the adult beetles may be removed. It takes about six months for the life cycle to be completed, so if you start your culture in the spring you should be assured of an adequate supply of mealworms throughout the following winter. Sub-divide your culture whenever possible, but don't discard the old food as it contains eggs and larvae. Do not allow excessive moisture to appear in the container, it may cause molds to appear or fermentation to start. When the mealworms are needed for your pets they can easily be removed by sifting the meal through a sieve. (The crushed newspaper or scraps of leather are added to the container to help relieve the pressure of the meal.)

Culturing Cockroaches

It is quite simple to raise cockroaches. With a little effort you should be able to maintain an adequate supply at all times. A large battery jar or similar sort of glass container with a tightly fitting screen cover will serve nicely. Cover the bottom with a layer of sawdust to a depth of a half inch or three-quarters of an inch. Place a small watch glass of drinking water in the sawdust so that its top is even with the sawdust. Now add your initial supply of cockroaches, which should be females carrying egg cases. You can obtain them from a local exterminator or from a supply house. When you have added the cockroaches place the container in a warm, dark place. Bread soaked in sweetened water, pieces of apple, cooked egg, and meat scraps, as well as cheese and various fruits are all satisfactory as food. But as cockroaches are omnivorous, other food items may be tried. Under favorable conditions you should have a good supply of cockroaches within a month. Allow some of the cockroaches to reach maturity. You can use them for breeding and start another culture. It might be advisable to place the battery jar or glass container in a shallow tray of water to prevent the roaches from escaping and taking up residence in your house.

Culturing Grasshoppers

Almost any type of container that permits the air to circulate is suitable for culturing grasshoppers. A gallon-size aquarium tank, a large battery jar, or screened terrarium will do very well. Cover the top with wire screening and the bottom with about two inches of soil. Put the grasshopper eggs in the soil at a depth of about one inch. Tamp the soil down firmly and sprinkle it with water. Sow grass seed in the rearing, or culturing, cage. The growing grass will help to maintain natural humidity and will furnish food for the emerging nymphs. Twigs or other supports should also be placed in the cage or terrarium. (You can buy grasshopper eggs from a supply house.)

If the eggs are obtained in the fall and kept at a temperature of 60 to 70 degrees Fahrenheit, they will hatch in January or February. The young nymphs will begin to eat about twelve hours after they have emerged from the eggs and will feed on the grass, as well as on almost any kind of vegetation. The grasshoppers will relish a lettuce leaf or a slice or two of apple dipped in water to provide moisture. Food left over from the previous day should be removed. After the nymphs have hatched, the cage or terrarium should be kept fairly dry. However, the grass should be sprinkled with water so that it will continue to grow.

Culturing Crickets

The black field crickets that serenade us during the summer may be kept in the same kind of container as that used for grasshoppers. As cricket eggs are laid in the fall and do not hatch until the following summer, it is best to lay in a good supply of crickets in late summer and early fall. As you use the crickets replenish the supply. Crickets can be purchased from a supply house or a cricket farm. The cage or terrarium should have a layer of soil and grass seed like that provided for the grasshoppers. Crickets can be fed a variety of foods: lettuce, moist bread, melon, and various fruits. To reduce cannibalism, it is advisable to give them bone meal.

Culturing Earthworms

It is relatively easy to raise and keep earthworms if a few simple precautions are observed. Earthworms keep best in a tight wooden box. The size depends on how many worms you want to raise. A box 18 x 36 x 60 inches, for instance, would be large enough for several hundred good sized worms. Fill the box with good soil which should be kept damp but not wet. The worms will require less artificial feeding if the soil is rich in humus. Do not use sandy soil. When the box is ready to receive the worms, collect them, either by digging for them or by merely walking around with a jar after a heavy rain and picking up worms from the surface of the ground or from a wet sidewalk. After you have collected an adequate supply, place the worms in the box, cover the surface of the soil with a layer of cut sod or, better still, with well-decayed leaves that will serve as a natural food for the worms. Moisten the soil from time to time, but don't add too much water. Keep the box in a warm place, but don't let the temperature get as high as 75 degrees Fahrenheit because heat will kill the worms.

The earthworms will live in the box for a long time and multiply rapidly. You should give them a little fat occasionally in the form of chopped beet suet, as well as crumbled hard-boiled egg or finely divided bread crumbs which may be sprinkled upon the surface of the soil beneath the leaves. Be careful not to let the food spoil as the worms may die.

RULES TO OBSERVE IN CARING FOR REPTILE PETS

Only by giving your reptile pets the proper care and attention will they be healthy and thrive.

Make it a habit to check the thermometer in the terrarium or cage.

Always maintain the proper amount of heat and light in the cage or terrarium.

Never place the cage or terrarium in direct sunlight, or if you do, be sure that only part of the cage or terrarium receives the sun's rays.

Desert lizards must always have a dry cage or terrarium.

Never pick up a lizard by its tail.

Never let anyone annoy your pets by tapping on the terrarium or cage.

Handle your pets as little as possible and never do so roughly.

41

Remember that lizards drink by lapping up drops of water from plants or other substrata and will not take water from a dish.

Don't give your chameleons a sugar and water diet.

Keep the woodland terrarium moist, but don't let it get too wet or soggy.

Be sure to provide twigs or other supports for climbing species.

If an aquarium tank is used as a terrarium be sure that the top is covered with wire screening.

Don't let your lizards get too hot or too cold.

Provide a layer of sand in the cage or terrarium for desert species.

Always offer your lizards live food except in certain cases.

Don't keep the cage or terrarium too near a window in the winter.

Don't neglect to sprinkle water on the plants or pieces of bark or other objects each day.

Be sure that the lizards, especially the desert forms, are not exposed to drafts.

Always provide some sort of shelter for your pets.

Don't make quick or sudden movements near your pets.

Be sure to start culturing earthworms, mealworms, etc., in time to have an adequate supply for the winter if you live in the North.

Under no circumstances keep a poisonous snake as a pet.

Remember that keeping reptile pets takes time and effort.

If, for any reason, you can no longer keep any of your reptile pets, do not turn them loose in a strange environment.

Be sure to keep the cages and terraria clean at all times; always remove uneaten food and always change polluted or foul water.

When feeding horned lizards, place them in the sun.

1

The Painted Turtle

A turtle makes a really nice little pet and is easy to keep, for it is an uncommonly hardy animal. A turtle is more responsive than you might think, soon getting to know you and learning to be hand fed.

The most familiar and beautiful turtle of the United States, where it ranges almost from coast to coast, is the painted turtle. It also occurs in extreme southern Canada. The painted turtle varies so much in appearance from one area to another that it has been given three subspecific names. (These are listed in the Appendix.)

Basking on a protruding stone or on a partially submerged log, ever alert to plunge into the water upon the approach of an enemy, the painted turtle adds a bright note to our ponds and streams.

It is an amusing sight to come upon three or four of these pretty reptiles sunning themselves on a rock or derelict timber and then, as the sound of footsteps reaches them, to see them tumble clumsily into the water. As soon as they touch the water, their broadly-webbed feet take hold and they quickly make for the bottom where they hide among the water plants. Should you

43

Fig. 13   Painted turtle

remain in the vicinity and watch quietly for their return, you will find that at first only snouts and eyes appear above the surface. In this manner they will swim about, inspecting the area for any possible sign of danger. When they are satisfied that all is safe, they will climb back one by one to their roost to resume their interrupted sunbath.

The painted turtle, the most common North American turtle, is not apt to be confused with other species. With its olive or blackish upper shell with the yellow-bordered shields and the striking crimson bars and crescents on the marginal shields and on both the upper and lower surface, it is perhaps the most beautiful North American turtle. The lower shell is an immaculate yellow, the head and neck are also spotted with yellow, and legs and the tail are marked with crimson (Fig. 13). Adult painted turtles usually reach a length of about five or six inches.

The painted turtle is commonly found in ponds and sluggish streams where the flow of water is not rapid and which contain an abundance of aquatic vegetation. It delights to paddle about the submerged water plants and chase small fishes, tadpoles, frogs, and the larvae of water insects that serve as its food. It is not a difficult turtle to capture and in captivity makes an excellent pet. Once its momentary fear has been overcome, it becomes quite tame.

The eggs of the painted turtle are pink in color and elliptical in shape. They are laid in a secluded spot during the latter part of June, invariably in the late afternoon or evening hours. The female selects a location (usually moist and sandy) near a body of water where she will deposit her half-dozen or so eggs, digs a hole, and then lays the eggs one after the other without turning around. She covers the hole so well that there is no telltale sign to indicate that there are turtle eggs there.

In its native environment, the painted turtle is active from early spring until October, when it digs down in the bottom mud of ponds and streams and hibernates until the warm days of returning spring call it forth once more.

The painted turtle should be kept in a semi-aquatic terrarium and may be fed chopped raw meat (meatloaf, chopped beef, steak), earthworms, raw chopped fish, and soft-bodied insect larvae. It should be fed at regular intervals, about once every two days.

Fig. 14   Spotted turtle

2

The Spotted Turtle

You will have no difficulty in recognizing the spotted turtle. The yellow spots, which are extremely variable in number, on its black upper shell and neck make it easy to identify (Fig. 14). Young spotted turtles, or hatchlings, usually have one spot in each large scute, but older turtles may be sprinkled with spots, sometimes numbering as many as a hundred. Conversely, the spots may be few or absent altogether, but this is rather rare. Because of its spots, the turtle is often referred to as the polka-dot turtle.

The spotted turtle occurs from southern Maine to extreme eastern Illinois and south in the East to Georgia. It is found in such habitats as marshy meadows, bogs, swamps, small ponds, ditches, or in various shallow bodies of water, often occupying the same places as the painted turtle. Its habits are somewhat similar to those of the painted turtle, but it is more leisurely in its movements and is rarely in a hurry. Unlike the painted turtle which plunges immediately into the water when alarmed, the spotted turtle takes its time in doing so and then hides itself in the mud or debris on the bottom. It has been known to make lengthy migrations on land, presumably to search for new feeding grounds or to seek a mate.

The spotted turtle has been used in studies on habit formation and seems to have done very well, profiting by experience and being able to learn quite rapidly. You might be able to think of various ways to test its learning ability.

Like the painted turtle, the spotted turtle should be kept in a semi-aquatic terrarium. It quickly becomes adjusted to captivity and will thrive with the proper care. In its natural habitat it feeds upon insects and insect larvae, worms, small mollusks, like snails, tadpoles, and dead fish, and it can be given any of these. It will also eat lettuce leaves. I have succeeded in getting it to take small pieces of raw meat.

47

Fig. 15   Snapping turtle

3

The Snapping Turtle

For a number of reasons probably no turtle is more familiar in the United States than the snapping turtle: its ferocity, great size, palatable flesh, and wide distribution. It is found from Southern Canada to the Gulf of Mexico, from the Atlantic Ocean to the Rocky Mountains, and has been introduced farther west.

A full grown snapper may weigh as much as forty pounds, but adults usually weigh between fifteen and thirty pounds and measure two or more feet long. (Gigantic individuals occasionally weigh from sixty to seventy pounds.) The upper shell varies in color from almost black to light horn brown and is sharply serrated on the rear. The tail is fairly long, twelve inches or more, and has a median dorsal crest of narrow plates. The head is unusually large with hooked jaws that are as dangerous as they appear. A medium-sized snapper can readily amputate a human finger, while a large specimen would not have much difficulty amputating a hand (Fig. 15).

The snapping turtle lives in any body of water large enough to support an association of aquatic plants: pond, lake, river, swamp, and salt marsh with a mucky, plant-grown bottom in which it often buries itself with only the eyes showing.

In water its form, color, and deliberate movements combine to make it inconspicuous, especially when the shell becomes camouflaged with plant growth. It is then a rather docile and inoffensive creature, and when stepped upon, as often happens, it usually pulls in its head and seems unwilling to attack the intruder.

On land, however, it becomes an entirely different animal, quick to defend itself and ready to attack anyone who might annoy it. At such times it becomes the very picture of ungovernable rage and will even advance to the attack. Sometimes the forward thrusts of the head may be so violent as to lift the turtle off the ground, if it misses the target.

The snapping turtle eats both plant and animal matter, including fishes, as well as many invertebrates, waterfowl, and carrion.

It spends the winter in the mud of ponds and streams, or in a hole in the bank from which it emerges anytime after April, earlier in the more southern parts of its range. After a period of courtship and mating, the female emerges from the water and rambles about on land in search of a nesting place. She usually selects soft, damp earth in which she digs a hole with her hind legs, and in which she lays twenty or more round, hard-shelled eggs about an inch in diameter.

As soon as the baby turtles have hatched they make for the nearest water. How they manage to find their way when the eggs are laid some distance from, and out of sight of, water is not known.

Adult snappers are far too dangerous to keep as pets but small ones three inches or so in length are perfectly safe. They are blackish or dark brown in color, with a light spot at the edge of each marginal scute. The carapace is very rough with three well defined longitudinal keels. The tail is as long or longer than the carapace.

Baby snappers should be kept in a semi-aquatic terrarium and may be fed small fishes, earthworms and raw meat. They may be fed four or five times a week, but the feedings can be increased or decreased according to the amount of food given and eaten.

4

The Wood Turtle

We usually associate turtles with water for they are often found in the vicinity of ponds and streams. But in the spring the wood turtle leaves the ponds and streams, where it hibernates in the muddy bottoms, and wanders through pastures, woodlands, and over upland fields. It may even appear in gardens and backyards.

The wood turtle has a beautiful carved or sculptured upper shell which makes it easy to identify. But we do not often see it because its gray-brown color helps to conceal it among the dead grasses and fallen leaves. With its hard shell the wood turtle hardly needs such protection, but protective coloration is of value to the turtlets because they are soft, defenseless, and sometimes too brightly colored. Infancy is the critical age in the life of all turtles because they are then easy prey to most of their enemies.

The shell of the wood turtle is very rough. Each large scute, in the form of an irregular pyramid, rises upward in a series of concentric grooves and ridges. There is some orange color on the neck and limbs, and at one time the wood turtle was called the redleg. Young wood turtles lack this orange color on the neck and limbs (Fig. 16).

The wood turtle occurs from Nova Scotia to eastern Minnesota and south in the uplands to Virginia.

Although the wood turtle is predominantly a vegetarian, it will eat animal matter and feeds on aquatic animals when in the

51

Fig. 16   Wood turtle

water and on various insects, slugs, snails, myriapods, earthworms, and crustaceans when on land. It appears to have a decided liking for mushrooms. We do not know how it distinguishes the poisonous kinds from the harmless ones. Perhaps it suffers no ill effect from eating the poisonous species. I have never seen it eat a harmful one. However, I have often seen it feed on wild strawberries. It is like catching the proverbial small child at the jam jar to come upon a wood turtle feeding on the berries, and then lumbering off through the underbrush, its mouth stained with the red juice.

Although turtles have well-developed middle and inner ears, they cannot hear in the ordinary sense of the word. But when courting and mating, turtles grunt and make other sounds. The male wood turtle utters a distinct yet subdued note, not unlike that of a tea kettle that is audible for thirty or forty feet. The female can emit a low whistle.

When mating, the male repeatedly whistles at the female, so presumably the whistling has sexual significance. But as mating takes place under water, the whistling seems to be part of a courtship gesture rather than an overt act to attract the attention of the mate.

The wood turtle is an alert, intelligent animal and with an unusual ability to learn. Experiments have shown that its behavior is about equal to that of various mammals. It is unexcelled among reptiles as a pet and is far more responsive than other turtles. When first captured the wood turtle is often shy, but it soon gets over its shyness and, once accustomed to captivity, will readily eat from its owner's hand. It will even beg for food, making known its wants by waving a leg or walking around in a circle.

During the summer the wood turtle may be kept outdoors in a grassy area enclosed with chicken wire. The area should be large enough so that the turtle or turtles have plenty of room in which to move about. They should be provided with some sort of retreat into which they may retire during the heat of the day. The enclosure should be located in a shady place or in one where it is shady for part of the day. In winter the turtles can be kept indoors in a heated room in a shallow wooden box containing a layer of soil. Like the outdoor enclosure the box should be sufficiently large so that the animals are able to move around. In captivity, the wood turtle will eat earthworms, chopped raw meat, various insects, slugs, snails, as well as sliced tomatoes, pieces of banana, lettuce, and berries. Water need not be provided. The turtles will get their liquid nourishment from the food they eat: Bananas, lettuce, and so on.

Fig. 17 Plastron of box turtle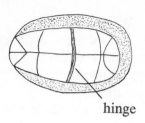

hinge

Fig. 18 Box turtles

5

The Box Turtle

The box turtle received its name because it is able to box itself in when alarmed or threatened with danger. Its lower shell or plastron is divided crosswise, the two parts fastened together by a hinge of cartilage. By means of a set of strong muscles the upper and lower shells can be closed together so neatly and so powerfully that it is extremely difficult, if not impossible, to pry them apart. They fit so closely that not even a knife blade can be inserted between them (Fig. 17). The shell provides adequate protection against all predatory animals, but some individuals become so fat from gluttony that they cannot withdraw completely within the shell and are exposed to attacks by rats and other voracious animals.

The box turtle, or more specifically the eastern species, is found from southern Maine to Georgia, west to Michigan, Illinois, and Tennessee. It measures, as an adult, from four-and-a-half to six inches in length and has a high, dome-like shell (Fig. 18) which is extremely variable in coloration and pattern. Both upper and lower shells may be yellow, orange or olive on black or brown, and either dark or light colors may predominate. In the male the rear lobe of the plastron has a central concave area, the eyes are sometimes red. In the female the plastron is flat or slightly convex and the eyes are normally brown. In the young the shell is much flatter, mostly a plain grayish brown, and each large scute has a spot of yellow.

Other species or subspecies are the Gulf Coast box turtle,

the Florida box turtle, the three-toed box turtle, and the ornate box turtle.

The box turtle is a land animal, though during the hot, dry spells of summer it seeks a muddy or watery place and soaks in the water or mud for hours at a time. It will even fall into a deep sleep which seems to be a form of aestivation, a state like hibernation that occurs during the summer. Box turtles will also burrow beneath a log or in rotting vegetation, however a heavy summer shower will usually bring them out of hiding.

The box turtle is primarily a woodland species but wanders into fields, meadows, and open areas adjacent to woods. In hilly regions, it prefers hillsides and other upland places, though it seems equally at home in flat country. We would not expect it to be adept at swimming, but some box turtles have been found that were rather good swimmers.

The box turtle feeds largely on vegetable matter, including berries. It is very fond of blackberries and gorges itself on them in late summer. It also eats the larvae of insects, slugs, adult ground beetles, and earthworms. On cool nights it will dig in for shelter under a log or big boulder. On the approach of winter it excavates a burrow in the ground about fifteen inches deep in which it hibernates until spring.

The eggs are thin and oval and are laid during June and July. They hatch in about three months.

The box turtle adapts itself readily to captivity and is probably kept more frequently as a pet than any other turtle. It may be kept in the backyard during the summer in an enclosure of chicken wire similar to that used for the wood turtle. Place a shallow pan of water in the enclosure for an occasional soaking. In the winter the turtle should be taken indoors and kept in a shallow wooden box in a heated room. It may be fed earthworms, sliced carrots, bananas, tomatoes, berries of various kinds, lettuce, and raw hamburger of which it is very fond. Box turtles have even been fed on table scraps. The box turtle has a fairly long life span. Ages of thirty and forty years are common, and some even reach the century mark.

6

The Musk Turtle

Few species of North American turtles are so widely distributed as the common musk turtle which is found in almost all of the eastern half of the United States, from southern Canada, south to the Gulf of Mexico and west to Wisconsin and Texas. Musk turtles are essentially southern forms. The common musk turtle is the only musk turtle found in the north, from southern Canada westward to Missouri.

The musk turtle is also known as stinkpot. The name refers to the yellowish fluid with a strong musky odor, that, at the time of capture, the animal exudes from two glandular openings on each side of the body where the skin meets the underside of the carapace. The secretion is defensive in nature, although the chief defensive tactic of the turtle is biting.

The common musk turtle rarely reaches a length of more than half a foot. Its oval-shaped upper shell varies from light olive-brown to almost black and is sometimes irregularly streaked or spotted with dark pigment. The lower shell has a single hinge. The leathery folds of skin of the legs are a purple-gray color, tinged with pink. Three characteristics distinguish the common musk turtle from other musk turtles: two light stripes on the head, barbels on chin and throat, and carapace scutes that do not overlap except in very young turtles. At times dark pigment may partly obscure the head stripes and in extreme cases the head may be uniformly black (Fig. 19).

The male common musk turtle can be distinguished from the female by the broad areas of skin showing between the scutes of the lower shell, or plastron, and a thick tail ending in a blunt, horny nail. The female has narrow areas of skin showing between the plastral scutes and a very small tail that may or may not have a

Fig. 19   Musk turtle

sharp horny nail. The young turtles have a black upper shell, or carapace, that is tough in texture with a prominent middorsal keel that gradually disappears with age, as well as light spots along the edge.

The common musk turtle is an abundant species yet we do not often see it. It is most at home in the mud of a quiet stream or in still water where the color of its shell blends with the bottom mud. Sometimes it is found in shallow clear water, leisurely patrolling the bottom in search of food and can be detected only if it is moving because the shape and color of its shell resemble that of a rounded stone. Sometimes the resemblance is heightened by the green algae that often grow on the shell. The algae are occasionally so dense that the animal becomes almost invisible and so secures a certain amount of protection against its enemies.

The common musk turtle also harbors on the lower shell, or plastron, stalked branched protozoans called opercularia. Frequently masses of protozoans cover the entire plastron, and with its upper shell covered with algae the turtle is a botanical garden above and a zoological garden below.

The most popular haunts of the common musk turtle are ponds and streams of various sizes. It also occurs in lakes, rivers, and ditches, and there are scattered records of it having been found in pools, lagoons, bayous, marshes, swamps, bogs, sloughs, and canals. It is an aquatic animal and rarely leaves the water except to nest. The sunning habit is poorly developed though specimens have been seen crawling out of the water and basking on a log or other projecting object. The turtle is more likely, however, to take the sun in shallow water with only part of its shell exposed above the surface.

The musk turtle eats small fish, insects, worms, and tadpoles. Though it is chiefly carnivorous, it sometimes eats water plants and other vegetable matter. It also acts as a scavenger and annoys fishermen by taking bait from a hook so gently that the angler is unaware that it has been stolen.

Most turtles show a remarkable uniformity in the selection of a nesting site: not so the common musk turtle which seems to find any place good enough. The female may make a crude nest or merely place her eggs, from one to five in number, almost anywhere—on top of a stump, in a bundle of rushes, in a cow track.

The musk turtle has a tendency to bite when captured or handled, so it is advisable to use a net when taking one in the water and always to hold the shell far back. It can be kept in a semi-aquatic terrarium or simply in an aquarium containing two or three inches of water. It may be fed insects and worms. I have succeeded in getting a musk turtle to eat raw meat like small pieces of beef steak or hamburger, which may be dropped in the water or given to the animal with a pair of forceps. Be sure that the water in the terrarium doesn't get dirty and foul; change it as often as is necessary.

Fig. 20   Carolina anole (American chameleon)

7

The Carolina Anole

Few of us have seen the true chameleon because it is found only in Africa, Madagascar, and India. But if you live in the South, in an area roughly from North Carolina southward through Florida and then westward into Texas, you need only to go outdoors at almost any time of the year (except during very cold periods) to see the American chameleon in trees, shrubs, and vines where it performs its repertory of acrobatics or engages in fighting, mating, or catching insects. This little lizard is often sold in pet stores, or circuses and carnivals (Fig. 20).

The American chameleon is not a chameleon and is only distantly related to the true chameleon. Because it undergoes the rapid color changes so typical of the true chameleon it is called a chameleon. More accurately it is an anole, and belongs to the genus *Anolis* of which there are some three hundred species and subspecies. Only two species occur within the boundaries of the United States: the so-called American chameleon, or Carolina anole, and the Key anole which lives on the island of Key West, Florida.

The Carolina anole is a somewhat ungainly animal. It has an overly large head that is quite distinct from the neck and a long, round slender tail. It measures about six inches in length. The male is a little larger than the female. But in spite of its awkward appearance the anole is far from clumsy. On the contrary, it is a most agile and active little animal.

This little lizard is an arboreal, or tree-dwelling, species. It

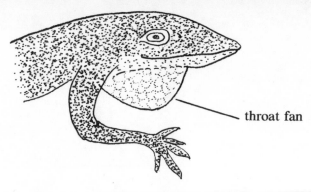

throat fan

Fig. 21   Carolina anole

has peculiar adhesive pads on its toes that help it to climb trees and shrubs. Look at the next to the last phalange, or joint, of a toe. The transverse, or crosswise, lamellae, or ridges, on the underside expand to each side to form a pad that enables the anole to cling to a smooth or vertical surface. The last phalange is normal in shape, that is, it is long and thin and ends in a claw.

A second unusual characteristic of the anole—one not shared by any other North American lizards—is the male's prominent throat fan or pouch which he can expand at will while nodding his head (Fig. 21). This throat fan is believed to be merely an ornament which serves no useful purpose. Perfectly flat when extended, it is exhibited only at mating or before fighting. It then becomes a vivid red, though occasionally it is orange or yellow. When two males fight, the encounter is invariably vicious and usually ends only when one of the contestants has lost its tail. However, this is no great catastrophe for the anole will immediately grow a new one. Although the new tail will not be exactly like the original, it will enable the animal to grasp, balance, and store fat.

To describe the color of the Carolina anole is rather difficult because the animal is not uniformly colored. Moreover, two specimens in the same situation may not have exactly the same color pattern. Most Carolina anoles are light brown above and flecked with brown below or are pure pale green above and white below. Between these two extremes, the animal can assume at will all the intermediate colors that can be imagined. For instance, the back may be mottled with brown and green or show irregular dark stripes. Dark species usually show several short longitudinal dark streaks on the sides of the throat and have fine white flecks and a spotting of darker brown on the sides of the body.

There is a popular, but erroneous, belief that the color changes, for which the American anole is famous, are influenced by the color of the animal's background, or by the color of the object on which it may be resting. This is not so. A green anole may often be seen on a weatherbeaten fence, or a brown one hopping from one green leaf to another.

Color changes are brought about by the way temperature and light influence the animal's activity, and by such emotional responses as anger and fear. Low temperatures induce a dark color whether the animal is in the shade or in the sun, but at high temperatures the color is controlled by various factors. When it is in the dark the animal is generally a green color, and shades of this green are associated with fighting and other emotional excitements. The animal is also green when asleep and/or dead; in the latter state scattered patches of black appear. Should the skin of your pet anoles suddenly begin to show dark spots and blotches, it may be a sign that the animals have been poorly fed and are weak.

Strictly diurnal in habits, the Carolina anole does not rise with the sun but waits until the morning is well advanced, and the temperature has risen. Then it leaves its perch, a twig well hidden among the leaves, on which it passed the night and goes on the prowl for flies, which it stalks like a bird and captures suddenly with a lightning-like thrust of its sticky tongue. The anole is quite at home among trees, shrubs, and vines, running at ease among the branches. Being a natural acrobat it often leaps from one leaf to another or on to some object to which it can cling by means of its adhesive foot pads.

During courtship rites and fighting, the animal may tumble to the ground in a breathtaking fall from which it makes an indignant recovery. It is not unusual for a male, when chasing a female, to leap two feet or more from one branch to another or to parachute to the ground from a height of thirty feet or more. The anole takes to water quite readily. If alarmed, when perched on a bush over a pond, it is just as apt to jump into the water and swim away as to escape by leaping through the branches.

The male anole stakes out an area, or territory, which he jealously guards and defends most vigorously, especially during the mating season. Should any male, at any time, attempt to invade his territory, the defending male will flare his dewlap and bob the forepart of his body in a series of push-ups, whereupon the intruding male will do the same or flee. If the intruder stands his ground, the threatening movements on the part of both males continue until the two come in physical contact and fight. The loser is banished from the area.

A male's territory may include the territories of several females with which he mates, and for which he may have to compete with other males. The breeding season extends from April to May. Mating is usually preceded by what is known as courtship behavior. When a male sights a female he displays his striking ruby-red throat fan and bobs his head. He then moves toward the female in short spurts, at the same time stopping to bob in a push-up fashion. The female then begins to hop about. If she is interested she stays fairly close to the male. Finally the male seizes the female by the neck in his jaws, and they mate.

The eggs, usually two in number, though there may be several clutches during the breeding season, are laid in trash piles or buried a few inches below the surface of the ground in loose, slightly moist debris. They hatch in six to seven weeks.

The Carolina anole is an amusing little animal and makes an excellent pet. It is also a good subject for studying lizard behavior. It has been known to live as long as three years in captivity. We do not know just how long it lives in the wild but it does not appear to live for more than a year or sixteen months at the most.

As the anole is a very active animal and likes to climb, run, and jump, it requires a large cage, at least two feet square, in which to move about freely. The cage can be a wooden box with an open side of fine-mesh screening, or it can be made entirely of screening as described in the section on housing. In any case, there should be a metal tray on the bottom for a layer of soil in which plants—ferns and the like—should be planted. Include a few twigs or perches on which the anole can climb and jump, and possibly some small lichen-covered rocks. Plants are essential because lizards drink by lapping up droplets of water scattered on the leaves. The plants must be sprayed with water, using a rubber bulb atomizer, at least once a day.

During the summer months, when insects are plentiful everywhere, you should have no problem feeding your anoles. Using an insect net, you can make one or two sweeps through the grass and other vegetation and collect enough insects for several feedings. A small piece of decaying fruit placed in the cage or terrarium will attract flies that will keep your pets from being hungry if you are unable to go outdoors on a collecting trip. In the winter you can feed your anoles mealworms or cockroaches that you culture. (See section on culturing.)

8

The Collared Lizard

The eastern collared lizard is not an appealing animal. It has a short and stout body with an uncommonly large head, hind legs that are larger than the front ones, and a very long round tail. Yet it is a colorful species, especially when outlined against the rocks where it usually lives. Its color is rather variable and may be yellowish, greenish, brownish, bluish, or a pale gray. Numerous white or yellow spots are scattered over its back and sides. At the edge of its abdomen these spots are often a brick red. There is also a series of slate-gray crossbands on its back. The abdomen is greenish, the throat a deep orange. The feature which gives the animal its name is the two black collar markings that pass around the throat and which are often broken at the nape of the neck (Fig. 22).

The female is similar to the male in color and markings, except that hers are less brilliant. Young collared lizards usually do not have the brilliant colors of the adults, and the markings are somewhat different. The neck collars are very broad, and the dark crossbands are more distinct and are black instead of gray. During the breeding season the adult male is more intensely colored than at other times. The bright colors are said to frighten away other males and to warn them to look elsewhere for a mate, though it doesn't always work out that way. At the same time the female develops bright brick red spots.

There are two other species of North American collared lizards—a western subspecies, which is very much like its east-

Fig. 22   Collared lizard

ern relative, and the reticulate collared lizard, one of the least known lizards, that lives only in extreme southern Texas and adjacent Mexico.

The eastern collared lizard occurs throughout the western states from Arkansas and Missouri to eastern New Mexico and southern Idaho and southward into Mexico. Its natural habitat is hilly, rocky, often arid or semi-arid country. It favors limestone ledges, rock piles where there are numerous hiding places, or open hillsides where there is little shade. It is seldom found on heavily shaded hills, flat prairies, or plains. It avoids large boulders. The collared lizard is not adept at climbing, finding nearly vertical sides difficult to ascend.

The collared lizard is a somewhat fierce animal and when startled will behave in a threatening manner. It appears to have excellent vision and can see an intruder at a considerable distance. It will then flee and seek cover. It is rarely taken by surprise. It moves in a curious way. When startled or frightened it will dart rapidly away, skimming over the ground in a normal lizard fashion, that is, running on all fours. Then as it gathers speed, it will lift its forelegs off the ground, raise its body and tail like a kangaroo, and run on its hind legs until it suddenly disappears into a crack in the rocks.

If cornered, or when escape is cut off, the lizard will turn quickly, open its mouth wide, revealing a black cavernlike throat, and if seized will bite readily. A cornered lizard will occasionally bite when being handled, which should be done as little as possible. The bite, while vicious, is not painful if it is on the fleshy part of the hand, but the reptile's small teeth can puncture the skin. If you are bitten by a collared lizard let the animal dangle freely. It will usually let go after a brief struggle. If you attempt to shake it off, it will tighten its grip. Do not grab its tail. If you do, the tail will probably break off, and you will have a permanently tailess lizard. The collared lizard, unlike most other lizards, is unable to grow a new one. Do not get the idea that the animal is a dangerous one. Far from it. A collared lizard is no more dangerous than your pet dog or kitten.

The collard lizard loves sunshine. Like most other species, it remains hidden during the night and early morning hours. It feeds on grasshoppers, spiders, beetles, and a variety of other insects. It also eats small lizards as well as other small vertebrates, so do not place such animals in the same cage as your collared lizard. It eats its prey in much the same way as a frog does, tucking the victim into its capacious mouth with its front feet. The collared lizard is also fond of flowers and will eat the blossoms of red clover and dandelion.

The female collared lizard lays from four to twenty-four eggs in loose sand to a depth of four or five inches or in tunnels underneath rocks. The eggs measure seven-sixteenths of an inch in diameter and five-eighths of an inch in length. Their covering is as thin and as soft as paper. The eggs hatch in nine to ten weeks and the young feed on insects like the adults.

The collared lizard is a hardy animal. If provided with the proper housing and given the required care, it does well in captivity. It should be kept in a desert terrarium like that described in the section on housing. A tropical fish aquarium will do nicely, except that the animal needs a very large one, which can be expensive. If you are handy with tools you can make one with little cost. A wooden box with a frame to support glass panels will also serve. Glass sides are essential to protect the lizards from cold drafts, which are harmful to all desert animals. The top should be covered with wire screening, not with glass. Glass creates a damp or humid atmosphere which desert animals cannot tolerate.

The terrarium should be placed where the lizards can get plenty of sunshine. Because the glass sides will concentrate the rays of the sun, making the terrarium unbearably hot for its inhabitants, you must not allow the temperature to get too high.

Attach a reliable thermometer to the inside of the terrarium and check it from time to time. A temperature of 75 to 85 degrees Fahrenheit should be maintained during the day, while 65 degrees Fahrenheit is permissible at night. Feed your lizards various kinds of insects. When insects are not available, substitute mealworms, cockroaches, or crickets which you can culture. If their natural surroundings are imitated as nearly as possible, and proper care given them, collared lizards should remain bright and healthy and give much pleasure.

9

The Fence Lizard

The popular name of an animal often tells us about some of its habits. The fence lizard's name suggests that it is often found on a fence. And it is, either sitting on a fence post or running along the rails. If you approach the animal, it will move to the opposite side and run along a rail for some distance, then stop and peer at you. If you stop, and then after a moment or two again move toward it, the lizard will repeat this behavior. Similarly, if the lizard is surprised on a log it will act in much the same way.

The preferred habitat of the fence lizard is dry, open, sunny woods, especially pine woods where it may be found in great numbers. Because it frequents pine woods, the fence lizard is also known as the pine lizard. It is often found in piles of logs, brush heaps, and similar places. It is quite adept at climbing, and trees and other objects on which it can climb are usually a feature of its environment. The fence lizard is seldom found far from protective cover where it can seek refuge when alarmed.

If you should come upon it on the ground and frighten it, it will dash for the nearest tree, climb the trunk for a short distance, then move to the opposite side where it will remain motionless. If you should move toward it from this side, it will climb still higher and again move to the opposite side, repeating the performance if necessary until it disappears from view.

The fence lizard belongs to a large and distinctive group of lizards known as the spiny lizards, or rough-scaled lizards. Their backs are covered with large, dull, keeled scales that end in sharp spinelike points. There are many species, but only one—the fence lizard—is found north of Florida or east of Texas. This species occurs in two forms, the northern fence lizard and the southern fence lizard. The northern fence lizard occurs throughout an area that extends roughly from southeastern New York, westward through northern Pennsylvania and central Ohio, southward through extreme eastern Kansas, the eastern fourth of Oklahoma and the eastern half of Texas, and in the east southward to northern South Carolina, then throughout the mountains and foothills west to Louisiana and eastern Texas. The southern fence lizard is largely restricted to the southern coastal plane of the United States.

The fence lizard is a rather small animal. A large northern male is about two and seven-eighths inches from snout to tail, a large female about three and one-quarter inches. The tail is about one-and-a-half times as long as the body.

The northern male is grayish brown with a series of seven to nine, occasionally six to ten, poorly defined narrow, wavy, slightly darker crossbands on the back. The broad, bright dark blue or green area at the base of the throat is often split in two parts. The sides of the belly are a bright blue or greenish blue bordered by black toward the center of the belly (Fig. 23).

The female tends to be more gray. The crossbands on her back are more distinct and her whitish belly is peppered with

Fig. 23   Fence lizard

black. Except for those differences the male and female are much alike in coloration. Young fence lizards resemble the female.

The southern fence lizard is similar to the northern except that it is slightly larger, with more brilliant markings; the black, especially, is more intense. In the male, the lower surface may be almost entirely black, except for patches of blue. In the female, the small black flecks on the belly are usually more numerous and are a little larger; in some instances they form a broken black line down the center of the belly.

The fence lizard feeds on spiders, insects, snails, millipedes, pseudoscorpions, and a variety of other invertebrates. It has a voracious appetite and prefers small and medium-sized insects. Once a captive lizard has become accustomed to a certain kind of food, it may take dead specimens as well as living ones.

In its own habitat, the fence lizard is attracted only by moving prey. It is able to see small objects at a distance of a few feet and notices anything that moves. It will detect the motion of an insect's antennae, if it is not too far away. It attacks its prey by making a sudden dash at the victim, seizing it, crushing it with its jaws, and then chewing and swallowing it. If the prey is long and bulky, the lizard will grasp it by one end, shake it into pieces, and then gobble up the separate fragments.

The fence lizard does most of its hunting early in the morning, following a brief sun bath, and may hunt again toward evening before seeking shelter for the night. On cool and cloudy days it may not venture forth at all.

The southern fence lizard remains active throughout the winter. But when cold weather begins to set in, the northern form disappears into an underground burrow, a retreat under or between rocks, or a refuge in a log or stump. There, secure from low temperatures and winter storms, the northern lizard hibernates until the following spring, or until the weather is once again warm.

Upon emerging from hibernation, the male fence lizards establish territories and guard them against other males. Fights are frequent, not only between the males that may be crowded together within a comparatively small area, but also between those that may wander from their own domain. The competition for females during the breeding season is often quite keen.

Once his mating instincts have been aroused, the male rushes toward the female, which he recognizes by her coloration, with a jerky, stiff-legged gait, his head and shoulders held high.

71

From time to time he pauses to bob up and down. The female moves away a short distance in a series of short, jerky hops while the male follows her. Finally he bites her on the neck or shoulders and, if she offers no resistance, mating takes place.

The female lays her eggs in a burrow which she excavates from one-half inch to four inches below the surface of the ground. She prefers sandy soil, but whatever site she selects must have sufficient moisture and warmth to incubate the eggs. The eggs, which number from four to seventeen, are oval and white, though later they become dingy. They measure one-half inch in width. They hatch in about ten weeks. Newly hatched young measure from thirteen-sixteenths of an inch to one inch.

The fence lizard does very well in captivity. A hardy species, it will live for several years if given the proper care. (In the wild the northern fence lizard is believed to live about eight years; the southern form, however, appears to have a life span of only a year or two.) The fence lizard may be kept in a woodland terrarium, which should be kept dry and provided with an abundant amount of sunlight. During the summer the fence lizard may be fed the various items listed earlier in this chapter. In the winter it can be given mealworms, crickets, and cockroaches.

If you watch your fence lizard carefully, you will observe that it changes color according to the temperature. For instance, in the sun the bright hues become a little brighter; in a cool temperature the dorsal pattern becomes much darker.

In a terrarium the fence lizard sometimes prefers to sleep on an inclined piece of wood rather than beneath a piece of bark or other cover. This behavior suggests that it may sleep in this way in the wild state, that is, at a slight distance above the ground and not under ground shelter.

The fence lizard is known to breed in captivity. Should you have a mating pair and the female lays eggs, they can be hatched by placing them in moderately damp but not soggy sphagnum moss at ordinary room temperature. The eggs hatch in eight to ten weeks.

10

The Horned Lizard

The curious-looking horned lizard is popularly, but erroneously, called the horned toad. There are twenty or more different kinds of horned lizards in the United States. Flat, large-bodied, short-tailed, and grotesquely horned, there are no others like them anywhere, except possibly for one odd Australian species known as the thorny devil.

The horned lizards are found in the western states where they inhabit almost any type of flat, dry land where there is little or no vegetation. They can be seen darting here and there in search of food during the hottest part of the day, fully exposed to the blazing sun. When they stop moving about, they seem almost to disappear, because they blend so well with the substratum on which they live. Long before the sun has set, while the heat waves still shimmer above the ground, they dig into the soil where they spend the night, using their noses like a plow and their heads like shovels. At times they may burrow as deep as two or three inches, at other times they bury themselves only deep enough so that the back is covered, while the head is just visible above the surface.

Probably the best known North American species of horned lizard is the Texas horned lizard. This lizard is sold in pet stores and is often carried home by tourists and visitors to the Southwest. Its name is somewhat misleading because it is not confined to Texas but occurs from Kansas, south through most of Texas, and westward through southeastern Colorado and southeastern

Arizona. It is a broad-bodied spiny species with a small, thin tail, two rounded central horns that rise sharply upward. The maximum head-body length is four and one-quarter inches (Fig. 24). Its color varies from a light yellowish-brown to a brownish-red or tan, though sometimes it is gray. Like most horned lizards, it has a very characteristic color pattern. A light middorsal line on the back extends from the head to the base of the tail with four rounded dark spots or blotches on each side; these spots are often edged in the rear with white or light gray. There is a large dark brown patch on each side of the neck. The several dark markings on the head may sometimes be indistinct. The lower surface is white or cream—sometimes yellowish-white—with a few dark spots on the belly.

With its armor of horns and spines, one would assume that the horned lizard is well protected against enemies, but birds like

Fig. 24   Horned lizard

hawks and roadrunners prey on it, as do whipsnakes and collared lizards, occasionally with disastrous results for the predator. Snakes have been found with a partially swallowed horned lizard whose horns were protruding through the skin of the neck.

When attacked by an enemy the horned lizard puffs itself out, tucks its head down, exposing the horns, and awaits its attacker.

The Texas horned lizard is far more active in the forenoon than at other times of the day and retires for the night in a burrow or under a flat rock, instead of burying itself in the soil. Like other horned lizards, it feeds on insects, especially ants, and small arthropods of various kinds. It does not capture its prey with a scampering rush, but somewhat like a toad, quickly extends its tongue once it gets close enough to an unsuspecting

74

victim. High temperatures are necessary to stimulate its appetite.

The Texas horned lizard goes into hibernation at the approach of the first cold spells in September or early October and does not reappear until the following spring in April or early May. Mating takes place shortly after the animal has emerged from its winter quarters. In late May or June the female lays twenty-three to thirty-seven eggs in a hole, five to seven inches deep. She excavates the hole with her forefeet, using the hind legs to push out the loosened soil. The eggs have a tough, leathery shell and measure about five-eighths of an inch in length and seven-sixteenths of an inch in diameter. They hatch in thirty-nine to forty-seven days. Some species of horned lizards give birth to live young.

When first captured, the average horned lizard appears rather spiritless. It seldom attempts to bite or show any resistance, although it may try to twist its head about to bring its horns in contact with its captor's fingers. It is apt to close its eyes and to give the impression of not caring what might happen to it. This behavior is possibly akin to playing possum. The horned lizard has the habit of voluntarily ejecting a stream of blood from its eyes. This is probably a secondary defensive weapon, though it also occurs during the time of skin shedding.

The horned lizard should be kept in a desert terrarium like that described in the section on housing. Sunshine and temperature are the two most important factors to consider in keeping horned lizards as pets. They need a flood of sunshine for the greater part of the day. Care must be taken that the temperature does not fall below 72 degrees Fahrenheit. If necessary a heater or electric light bulb should be placed in the terrarium to maintain the required temperature. The horned lizards should be fed small insects of various kinds, preferably ants, but during the winter when ants are not obtainable in the North, insects such as crickets and mealworms must be substituted.

If confined too closely, male horned lizards will fight in hot weather. Their fighting is rather harmless and usually consists of nothing more than a great deal of puffing and blowing. The horned lizard cannot break off its tail when it is grasped. In fact this is one lizard that can be captured by grasping its tail.

You can hypnotize a horned lizard by stroking it gently three or four times between the eyes. It will then close its eyes and become very quiet, even losing some of its reflexes.

Figs. 25 & 26   Five-lined skink

11

The Five-lined Skink

The five-lined skink has possibly the widest distribution of any North American lizard. It occurs from southern New England, south to northern Florida and westward to southeastern South Dakota and central Texas. Anyone who lives in the eastern half of the United States can go into the woodlands and expect to see this lizard in its natural surroundings.

The five-lined skink (Figs. 25 & 26) is found in wooded areas, especially in cut-over woodlots with an abundance of rotting stumps and logs, in abandoned sawdust piles, rock mounds, and masses of decaying debris. It is diurnal in habits. When the temperature is high it may often be seen basking on a log or stump or stretched out in dry leaves on the ground. It is an extremely nervous animal and does not remain in one place very long. It always has a retreat near at hand and at the slightest noise will quickly disappear into it. A few moments later, it will poke its head out to see what kind of danger threatens, for it has an insatiable curiosity.

With the setting of the sun, the five-lined skink seeks a sheltered place in which to spend the night. It may be a burrow under a fallen tree or a cavity in the trunk itself. The animal doesn't like cool weather. When the temperature is low it remains well sheltered. It never wanders far from its retreat even when foraging for food. Its diet consists of various small insects, earthworms, spiders, the eggs of birds, and newly-born wood mice that it often comes upon when investigating the crevices of a fallen tree. When alarmed it immediately flashes out of sight, whereas other lizards run for a distance and then stop and peer back to discover the source of their alarm.

Young five-lined skinks, which measure up to four or five inches in length, are more or less uniformly jet black with a central white or yellowish stripe that forks on the head and two similar stripes on each side. The stripes extend to the tail where they are lost in a shade of brilliant blue. The young skink is sometimes called the blue-tailed lizard.

As the young grow and become older, the striped pattern becomes less conspicuous and distinct. The black gives way to a dull brown, the stripes fade while the tail loses all trace of blue. The females almost always retain some indications of the striped pattern. Though the males usually show faint traces of the stripes, they become more nearly a uniform brown or olive. At the same time, the head turns a reddish color, fiery red in the male but less pronounced in the female. The male's head also becomes wide and swollen at the temples, giving the animal a mean and ugly look. Because of the color of its head the male is often called the red-headed skink.

The five-lined skink hibernates during the winter in a retreat like a rotten log, a sawdust pile or in the ground, emerging in the spring when the weather becomes warm. Shortly after it reappears, mating takes place. The male begins his courting ritual by first making a few scratching motions with his hind legs. Then he rushes with open mouth toward any member of the species that may be nearby and bites it on the neck. Should this lizard fight back—an action that indicates it is a male—the courting male loosens his grip and repeats his performance with another, and possibly with still another, until he finds one that does not resent his advances, and which is then identified as a female.

The eggs are laid in clutches of from two to eighteen. Smaller clutches are laid by small females, the larger by large females. They are deposited in rotten logs or in loose soil and are brooded by the female. The brooding, an unusual lizard trait, protects the eggs from being eaten by other lizards, even those of the same species. The mother might eat her own eggs should she become sufficiently hungry, though as a rule, during the incubation period, which lasts about six weeks, she takes time off for an occasional sunbath or to go in search of food.

The five-lined skink makes an unusual and interesting pet and does very well in captivity. As it is a fairly large lizard, measuring in total length about nine inches, it requires a large cage or terrarium, preferably a glass terrarium rather than a screen cage as drafts are harmful to lizards. The terrarium should contain a layer of soil. Cover the soil with dead leaves, and add several pieces of bark to provide a hiding place. The five-lined skink will eat almost any kind of small insect, and in the winter, mealworms, cockroaches, and the like, which can be cultured.

A word of caution. When handling the skink be careful. The animal will invariably attempt to bite and unless held in the proper manner may succeed in doing so. Usually a skink's teeth cannot penetrate the skin, but its pinch can be a painful one. A skink bite is not poisonous. Do not become alarmed if the animal should manage to take hold of your hand or fingers; it will soon let go.

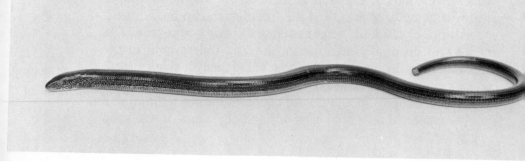

Fig. 27   Glass lizard

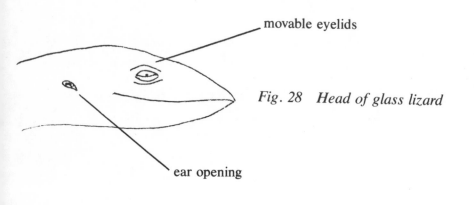

movable eyelids

Fig. 28   Head of glass lizard

ear opening

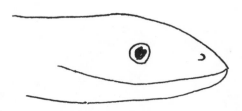

Fig. 29   Head of snake without movable eyelids or ear openings

12

The Glass Lizard

The glass lizard (Fig. 27) may not make as interesting a
pet as some other lizards, but it is an unusual animal in many
respects, and so you might want to include it among your other
reptile pets if you are able to obtain one. It is a southern species,
occurring from North Carolina to Florida and west to Louisiana.
You will have to buy a specimen from a reptile dealer unless you
live in the South.

The glass lizard gets its name from the old belief that if
struck the lizard will shatter like a piece of glass. An even more
preposterous variant of this myth is that after being broken into
numberless pieces, the animal will gather all the pieces together
and reconstitute itself into its original form.

There is a grain of truth to this bit of fiction, as there is to
most folklore. Like most other lizards, the glass lizard is able to
break off its tail and to grow a new one. But in the glass lizard this
ability is probably of greater value than it is to other lizards. The
glass lizard doesn't have any legs and is unable to move quickly or
to run away when confronted with danger. The broken piece of
tail has an extraordinary reflex action and will wriggle vigorously.
An enemy or predator that seizes the lizard's tail is very apt to be
distracted by the writhing fragment in its grasp, and to let the
lizard escape. The tail is very likely to break into several pieces,
each of which has the same degree of reflex action.

When the lizard is captured by hand and held up, it will twist
violently and break the tail into several pieces so that it literally

seems to be shattered. This probably accounts for the myth that the lizard shatters like glass. The tailless body may be only a third of the entire length of the animal and can be mistaken for just another piece of tail. Whenever the glass lizard loses its tail, it grows a new one, which is usually shorter than the original though it still serves its purpose. You will rarely find a glass lizard with its original tail.

The glass lizard is often called the glass snake. It is a long, slender, shiny, legless animal with a tail considerably longer than its body and might easily be taken for a snake. But look at it carefully and you will find that it has movable eyelids and external ear openings (Fig. 28) which snakes do not have (Fig. 29). To the touch it feels stiff and hard, brittle, and completely lacks the suppleness of a serpent. An identifying characteristic is the deep flexible groove or fold along each side of the body which permits the body to expand when filled with food and, in the case of the female, when filled with eggs.

There are three species of glass lizards in the United States, and they are all rather confusingly alike. The species with the widest distribution is the slender glass lizard, which occurs from southwestern Virginia to southern Florida, west to central Texas, and north in the Mississippi Valley to eastern Kansas, southern Wisconsin, and the dune region of northern Illinois and Indiana. It may be recognized by its legless condition, a middorsal dark stripe, and the series of narrow, longitudinal stripes below the lateral groove (or fold) and under the tail. The stripes are black in the young but paler and less distinct in the adults.

The eastern glass lizard, which is a southern species, is an inhabitant of wet meadows and grasslands and pine flatwoods; the slender glass lizard lives in dry grasslands or dry, open woods. It is somewhat shy and retiring and is often found beneath litters of dead leaves and other debris. It is capable of burrowing, but does not burrow often or as much as the eastern glass lizard or the third species, the island glass lizard, which is found in coastal areas and on the offshore islands of South Carolina, Georgia, and Florida. It is a diurnal animal although there is some evidence that it may be active by night. Observe it closely and you will find that it moves over the ground by means of lateral undulating movements that are stiff and clumsy, quite unlike the more graceful ones of the snake. It may sometimes be seen basking in the sun.

The eggs, which number from eight to seventeen, are laid

from early June through July and are brooded by the female under cover, but such parental care does not extend to the newly hatched young. The glass lizard has very little protective instinct during the period of incubation and on being disturbed will immediately take flight, leaving the baby lizards to fend for themselves.

Glass lizards feed on insects, spiders, snails, birds' eggs, and small snakes and lizards. In captivity they will usually accept a mixture of chopped raw meat and egg. As they are fairly large animals, measuring as much as three feet or more, they require fairly large quarters. Their terrarium should have a layer of gravel or soil, covered with dead leaves, in which they can burrow and under which they can hide.

Fig. 30   Six-lined race runner

13

The Six-lined Race Runner

If you live within its range, which extends from Maryland south to the Florida Keys, west to southeastern Wyoming, eastern Colorado and Texas, and north in the Mississippi-Missouri Valley to Lake Michigan, Wisconsin, and South Dakota, you need only go outdoors on a sunny day to any of its habitats, and you are likely to see a six-lined race runner. It prefers open well-drained areas that are covered with sand or loose soil, such as fields, open woods, margins of thickets, flood plains, and rocky outcrops. The essential factor that determines whether this lizard occurs in any given area appears to be dryness. It is more apt to be found in a place where the soil is loose and porous rather than loamy. Though it avoids dense vegetation, it can be found in regions with low-growing plants and shrubs that do not require moisture.

There is no mistaking the six-lined race runner. It has a slender and graceful build, with strong limbs, a long whiplike tail, and a well-defined pattern.

There are several species of race runners in the United States, but only one, the six-lined, occurs east of the Mississippi River. It is one of the smallest of the race runners (Fig. 30), measuring about ten inches in total length, of which about two-thirds is tail. Its name comes from the six narrow light longitudinal lines or stripes, which may be white, yellow, pale gray, or pale blue, on a brown ground color, that extend from the head to the base of the tail. In adult males these lines or stripes are less distinct than in the females and young. The sexes can be distinguished by the color of the belly, that of the male being blue, that of the female white. The young have a light blue tail.

85

The six-lined race runner prefers a locality that is sunny with an adequate cover of stones, logs, boards, and the like, or one with holes and burrows, which may be those of a mammal or of its own making. It uses the burrows as a retreat during the night and on cool days and lays its eggs in them. Its diet consists of insects, though it also eats other arthropods and snails. The lizard feeds in the morning and again in the evening, spending the hottest part of the day beneath a low bush or other low growth or in a burrow.

The race runner is an active species and requires rather large quarters when kept as a pet. It is a bold animal and at times can be almost defiant, going about its business even though watched by an observer who keeps his distance. If you should be the observer and move closer (less than fifteen feet) toward it, the lizard will stop whatever it is doing and look at you with a wary eye. If you persist in coming still closer, it will immediately seek the nearest cover. Should you by any chance decide to chase it, you will quickly discover why it is called the race runner, or fieldstreak. You are not likely to catch it, for this lizard can attain a speed of eighteen miles an hour. However, as it has the habit of entering small holes or crevices, you can easily dig it out if you see into which hole it has disappeared. It is not arboreal, that is, it does not climb trees or bushes.

The race runner spends the winter in a burrow, retiring there when the temperature drops to a low average and not reappearing until the following spring, usually in April. Mating takes place within two or three weeks after it emerges from its winter retreat, and a regular courtship pattern is followed. The male apparently is unable to recognize a female. He will make advances to whatever individual he happens to meet, turning to others when his advances are rejected, until at last he finds a receptive female.

Four to six eggs are laid, four to twelve inches below the surface of the ground, frequently under some object like a log. Sometimes the female uses the tunnel of a mole in which to lay her eggs, first excavating a small side tunnel for her nest. The eggs hatch in August.

Race runners do well in captivity if given the proper care. As they are quite active and measure from six to nine inches long, though some large specimens have attained a length of seventeen inches, they require, fairly large quarters. A large tropical fish aquarium will do nicely. It should have a layer of sand, not woods soil, into which the lizards can burrow and some form of cover beneath which they can retire.

As these lizards feed essentially on insects they may be given grasshoppers, crickets, ants, flies, caterpillars, and the like. They seem to prefer soft-bodied insects and usually reject hard-bodied species like beetles. During the winter it is advisable to have a supply of crickets always available. You can culture crickets following directions in the section on culturing insects.

The race runner has a forked tongue which it moves in and out of its mouth in the manner of a snake. Most lizards do not have a forked tongue, and those that do are more sparing in its use, keeping it in the mouth and slowly flicking it out only when they want to determine the character of some object, such as food, that they have under scrutiny.

Fig. 31 Green Grass Snake

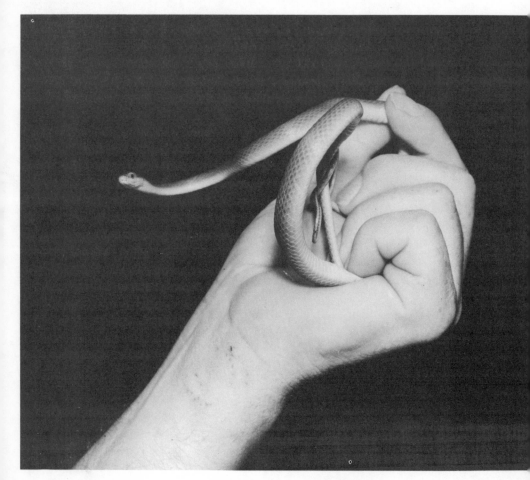

Fig. 32 Green Grass Snake

14

The Green Grass Snake

The green grass snake (Figs. 31 & 32) is a docile and gentle animal.

As its name indicates, the green grass snake is green in color and occurs in grassy places. It is bright green above and white, washed with yellow, below. The scales are smooth with a satiny luster. The lips have the pale tint of its lower surface. Freshly hatched young are dull olive above and are from four to six and one-half inches long; fully grown adults measure about fifteen inches.

The green grass snake occurs in Canada from the Maritime Provinces to southern Manitoba. In the United States it is found in the East to northern New Jersey and in the mountains to North Carolina; in the West to Texas and New Mexico. It is an upland snake in the eastern and far western parts of its range, but it occupies the lowlands in the north-central regions.

Open fields and fence rows are this snake's normal habitats. It usually stays on the ground, crawling slowly through the grass, though occasionally it climbs into bushes and vines where it coils itself among the stems and tendrils. Its green color blends so well with its surroundings that it is difficult to detect. And one comes upon it more by accident than by intent. It will remain motionless on a bush or vine, but if disturbed, when moving through the grass, will take off with bewildering speed. Toward the latter part of the day it will often crawl under a flat stone that has been warmed by the sun.

The green grass snake is insectivorous in its feeding habits, eating crickets, grasshoppers, katydids, and particularly the green hairless caterpillars that are found in the areas where the snake occurs. These caterpillars are the larvae of certain moths and measure about an inch in length and slightly less than a quarter of an inch in thickness. The snake will also eat spiders.

The green grass snake lays its eggs in August under flat stones and logs or in sawdust piles. They are elongate in shape and have such a thin covering that they can be dented by the slight pressure of a finger. The eggs are so translucent that the dark embryos can be seen in them just before hatching. No more than a dozen eggs are laid at one time. The short incubation period never lasts more than twenty-three days. Therefore most of the development of the young occurs before the eggs are laid.

The green grass snake will submit to the most vigorous handling without showing the slightest anger; even when newly captured it will not make any attempt to escape. I have never been bitten by one and have never heard of a green snake biting anyone.

For this reason, and because it requires little care, the green snake makes an ideal pet.

It should be kept in a woodland terrarium and fed the insects that are its normal diet. In captivity it will also eat cockroaches which you can obtain from a local exterminator or rear yourself. It is advisable to rear your own cockroaches, as well as crickets, so that you will always have a food supply for your pet, especially during the winter when other insects are not obtainable. Occasionally the snake can be made to grab a small piece of raw beefsteak dangled at the end of a long thread, but it takes a little time and patience to get it to do so.

15

The Brown Snake

One of the easiest, if not the easiest, snakes to obtain for a pet is the brown snake because it is found everywhere, in the city as well as in the country. In the city you can find it in almost any park, cemetery, or vacant lot, and it might well be called the city snake. In the country you can find it in any of its normal habitats—bogs, swamps, freshwater marshes, moist woods, hillsides—in fact almost any place. It sometimes even turns up in backyards.

But finding it is another matter. The brown snake is very secretive and hides during the daylight hours beneath flat stones, the bark of trees, logs, and trash of all kinds, including old linoleum and roofing. The brown snake was at one time known as DeKay's snake, after James Edward DeKay, an early New York naturalist. It is a most inoffensive little animal. When frightened or alarmed, it flattens its body and emits a fluid that has a musky odor. This is the only means the snake has to defend itself.

The brown snake rarely exceeds twelve inches in length. It has a moderately stout body with heavily keeled scales and large eyes. It is a rather drab chestnut or grayish brown, though sometimes it is dark brown or reddish brown. There is a clay-colored stripe down the middle of the back, bordered more or less with small black spots. A distinguishing feature is the downward streak on the side of the head (Fig. 33). The young are darker in color than the adults and have a conspicuous yellow collar across the neck. They measure from three and three-eighths to four and one-half inches. Their dark color changes

Fig. 33   Brown snake

rapidly and during the warm months following the first hibernation becomes that of the adult.

The brown snake is found in southern Canada and in the United States east of the Rocky Mountains whence it extends southward into Mexico.

This little snake spends the day in a safe retreat, emerging during the late afternoon to feed. It is then often seen crossing a country road. It feeds largely on earthworms and slugs, but will also eat small salamanders and the soft-bodied grubs of beetles.

The brown snake is viviparous, that is, it gives birth to live young. The female will produce from twelve to twenty young 105 to 113 days after mating, birth occurring the latter part of summer. The birth of a brood may take from one to several hours, with some time elapsing between successive births. The young snakes become quite active very soon after they are born.

The brown snake makes a very nice pet. It is easy to care for and does well in captivity. It may be kept in a woodland terrarium like that of the green grass snake. It is essential that it be provided with a flat stone or piece of bark under which it can hide. It should also have a dish of water that should be changed every day. Water is most important to snakes as they cannot live without it. Watch the brown snake drink—it drinks like a horse.

Feed it earthworms and the food it eats when in its natural habitat. It is advisable to keep a supply of earthworms during the winter. Direction for rearing earthworms are given in the section on culturing.

16

The Garter Snake

The garter snake is perhaps our most common species. It is the most widely distributed and abundant of our harmless snakes. The eastern species, of which we write, occurs from southern Canada to the Gulf of Mexico and west to Minnesota and eastern Texas. It is found in almost every kind of habitat, is fond of both dry and damp places, and is at home equally in a bog, marsh, field or pasture, as well as in a garden and backyard. It is a sun-loving animal and you will often come upon it lying in the sun in open spaces as you stroll along a country road or follow some woodland path (Figs. 34 & 35).

The garter snake varies in color, but in general it has three yellowish or greenish stripes against a ground color of brown, green or black. There is usually a double row of alternating black spots between the stripes. It is not a particularly large snake. An extremely large specimen will measure about three feet in length. It is very hardy. It is the last to hibernate in the autumn and the first to appear in the spring. In early March, even though patches of snow still remain on the ground, large numbers of garter snakes can be seen in open sandy areas getting the full benefit of the sun. Then as soon as the sun begins to sink in the western sky, they return to their winter shelter among the clefts and fissures of rocky sites.

They remain in and about their hibernating quarters until the weather has settled and the need for shelter has passed, then they mate and scatter. The garter snake brings forth its young alive.

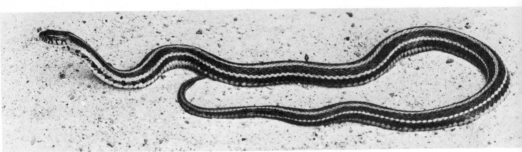

Figs. 34 & 35   Garter snake

The young, about six inches long at birth, are born in July and August and may number from a dozen to fifty. They immediately shift for themselves. They feed on earthworms, although they will also eat small toads and insects. If all goes well and they are not captured by a predator or small boy or girl, they will mature in about a year's time.

As the cold weather of autumn approaches, garter snakes begin to gather in groups in places suitable for their winter's sleep. Here they sun themselves during the middle of the day, retiring into clefts and fissures among rocks, or into burrows on chilly nights, and moving into them permanently for the winter after the first severe frost.

The garter snake is not a vicious reptile by any means. Like most reptiles, if danger threatens, it will seek an avenue of escape, but if cornered will put up a stubborn fight. When first captured, a garter snake exudes a strong and offensive odor from glands at the base of the tail, but after a few days of captivity it discards this disagreeable habit. It does well in captivity and makes an excellent pet, becoming quite tame and docile.

An aquarium filled with a layer of soil and covered with wire screening or a cage such as that described in the section on housing will do nicely for quarters. In the wild state, its food consists largely of earthworms, frogs and, insects, but I have succeeded in getting a garter snake to eat raw meat. In time, with good food and kind treatment the snake will learn to associate your hand with food and will take it from your fingers without trying to bite.

Fig. 36   Northern (or common) water snake

17

The Water Snake

I first became acquainted with water snakes when one morning many years ago I decided to go down to the river not far from where I lived to do some fishing. Just as I reached the water's edge, a water snake that had been sunning itself on an overhanging branch of a water beech struck viciously at me. It missed, but if it had bitten me it would not have mattered. The snake is harmless and can inflict only a superficial bite. It looked quite sinister as it glared at me with its beady eyes, but actually the reptile has no heart for fighting. It will fight if cornered, as any animal will, but given a chance to escape it will quickly take advantage of it. When, startled, I retreated a step or two, the water snake dropped into the water and disappeared in the river.

There are several species of water snakes. The one I encountered was the northern water snake, which occurs from southern Maine, extreme southern Quebec to North Carolina and the southern uplands and west to Colorado. This snake is a rather large species, from two to three feet or more long, and varies in coloration. It has dark crossbands on the neck and forepart of the body with alternating blotches on the top and sides of the rest of the body. The dark markings are wider than the spaces between them, and there are black or reddish half-moons on the belly. The ground color varies from pale gray to dark brown, the markings from bright reddish-brown to black. As the snake grows older the colors often tend to darken so that the pattern becomes less distinct and may disappear entirely, leaving the snake a plain black or dark brown. The half-moons on the belly may be arranged in a regular pattern, or scattered at random, or be merely dusky areas. They may even be absent altogether. You may find some specimens with their bellies almost uniformly stippled with gray except for a yellow, orange or pinkish stripe. The young, which measure from about seven and one-half inches to nine inches at birth, have black crossbands on a ground color of pale gray or light brown (Fig. 36).

The water snakes are semi-aquatic snakes. They are often seen basking on logs, branches, or brush from which they drop or glide into the water at the slightest alarm. The northern water snake may be found in virtually every pond, lake, stream, marsh, swamp, or bog within its range, preferring quiet waters but not adverse to living in swift-flowing streams and even in the vicinity of waterfalls. All water snakes are adept at swimming and diving. They obtain most of their food, such as frogs, salamanders, fish, and crayfish, in or near the water. Though they are harmless, water snakes have been greatly maligned and are feared more than any other non-poisonous species because they strike and bite viciously when cornered. Then, too, they are resented because of the mistaken belief that they prey on fishes. It has, however, been shown that they actually improve fishing by culling out the sick and less desirable fish. They help reduce the population in ponds and lakes that contain such an overabundance of fish that the crowded fish would be stunted in size. Water snakes bring forth their young alive. Those of the northern water snake are born in August and September in a brood containing twenty or more.

As adult water snakes may be vicious in temperament they are not altogether desirable as pets. However, the young are quite docile and do well in captivity. They should be kept in a fairly large woodland terrarium, which is provided with a pan of water, and may be fed earthworms, canned sardines, and raw chopped fish.

18

The Ring-necked Snake

If you have never kept a snake as a pet it might be advisable to begin with the ring-necked snake, for, with the exception of the green grass snake, you will never find a more docile, inoffensive snake. Moreover, in its different species, it occurs in almost every part of the United States as well as parts of Canada. And it is easy to recognize with its slate-colored back, black-bordered yellow, red or orange band just behind the head, and predominantly orange or yellow belly (Fig. 37).

The ring-necked snake is a small species, measuring when full grown about fifteen to twenty inches in length. It lives in wooded areas, most commonly in cutover areas, but it is also found in rocky wooded hillsides. Nocturnal and secretive, it lives under stones, in and under decaying logs or rotting wood, as well as under the loose bark of fallen trees. Sometimes a number of ring-necked snakes may be found together in a single log. Some ring-necked snakes have the rather curious habit of curling the tail when annoyed and exposing the brilliant colors of the lower side. Possibly this is an attempt to bluff their way out of danger.

The diet of this small snake is surprisingly varied and includes earthworms, insects, frogs, salamanders, lizards, and even other snakes—all of which you can feed it. The ring-necked snake feeds at night so you will not often observe it eating. It should be kept in a woodland terrarium.

Most small snakes, and the ring-necked snake is no exception, are at times difficult to keep, but they do make attractive study specimens. Success in keeping any snake as a pet depends on the care you give it.

Fig. 37   Ring-necked snake

19

The Hog-nosed Snake

Spread-head, blow-snake, puff adder, hissing viper, all are names of what is probably the most notorious and widely feared of North American snakes.

Despite these fearsome names, the snake is completely harmless and cannot be induced to bite whatever the provocation. Then why is it so feared? Because it is a most capable actor and, when encountered for the first time, can deceive almost anyone.

The names listed above are some of the names given to a serpent usually known as the hog-nosed snake because of its upturned snout. It is stout of body, slow-moving, and superficially viperish in appearance. Its general coloration varies. The predominate color may be yellow, brown, gray, orange, or red. Normally it is a spotted snake, but jet-black specimens or nearly plain gray ones occur in some areas. The belly is mottled, gray or greenish on yellow, light gray or pink. It measures from eighteen to thirty inches in length (Figs. 38 & 39).

There are several species but the one described here is the eastern species and is perhaps more accurately known as the eastern hog-nosed snake. It is found from New Hampshire to southern Florida and west to South Dakota and Texas.

The hog-nosed snake is found in dry, sandy situations, often on a dusty country road, but it may on occasion get into a garden or backyard. Toads are its chief food, but it will also eat frogs and tadpoles and some kinds of insects, though insects are more likely to be eaten by the young snakes.

Southern hog-nosed snake (middle)

Fig. 38 Eastern hog-nosed snakes (top and bottom)

Fig. 39 Hog-nosed snake

Unlike other snakes that silently glide away when approached by an intruder or an enemy, the hog-nosed snake does not seek to escape but holds its ground, flattening and spreading its head and the forepart of its body to twice their normal size, in the manner of the cobra, and bringing into view other colors. At the same time, it inflates its lungs to capacity with air which it then expells with a loud hiss. Should you approach it ever so closely, it will strike out at you, but always with its mouth closed. Its teeth are rarely brought into play. This fearful display of ferocity will strike horror in anyone seeing it for the first time. It is a most amazing performance and is all sheer bluff. Were you to reach down, as if to take hold of it, the snake might hit your hand, but it would not bite it.

This is not the extent of the hog-nosed snake's acting ability. If it is further molested, it opens its mouth wide, sticks out its tongue, contorts its body, writhes as if in agony, covers itself with all sorts of dirt and debris, and sometimes even becomes bloody. It then rolls over on its back and lies perfectly still as if dead. Pick it up and it will hang limp and apparently lifeless in your hand and remain that way even though you handle it somewhat roughly. But should you roll it over on its belly or place it on the ground right side up, it will immediately turn over on its back again. If you completely ignore it and retreat a few steps, it will, if left undisturbed for a few minutes, raise its head and, seeing no danger, crawl away.

The hog-nosed snake is not the only snake that will play possum in order to escape from a potential enemy. There are other snakes in various parts of the world that put on a similar act, but none gives a performance that can compare with that of the North American species.

It is somewhat difficult to tell how effective such behavior is, because we know little of its effect on other animals. The effect on human beings of this apparent show of hostility has earned for the hog-nosed snake a widespread and unwarranted evil reputation.

Strangely, after a short period in captivity the snake loses this unique and remarkable ability, and it becomes virtually impossible to get it to go through its act.

The hog-nosed snake is actually a gentle harmless creature and does well in captivity. It should be kept in a fairly large cage like that described in the section on housing. It has a voracious appetite and feeds on frogs and toads. It is therefore somewhat difficult to keep through the winter unless you can obtain these animals from a supply house. It might be best to put the snake outdoors when cold weather approaches so that it can find a snug retreat in which to hibernate for the winter.

The hog-nosed snake mates in April and May, and the eggs are laid in June or early July. They vary in number from eight to forty or more and measure about one and one-quarter inches by seven-eighths of an inch. Hatching occurs from July to September, the young measure six and one-half to eight inches in length.

20

The Common Caiman

At one time young or baby alligators were sold to tourists and in the pet trade, but today the alligator is protected by law and is no longer available as a pet. Neither is the crocodile. Caimans, however, can be obtained as pets at the present time, but some day, they, too, will probably be considered an endangered species. No animal can be hunted indiscriminately without being threatened with extinction.

The caimans, which are closely related to the alligators, are found from the Isthmus of Tehuantepec to southern Mexico to northern Argentina. There are five species: the black caiman, the broad-nosed caiman, the smooth-fronted caiman, the dwarf caiman, and the spectacled caiman. The spectacled caiman is divided into four subspecies or geographic races, namely the brown caiman, the Apoporis River caiman, the Paraguay caiman, and the common caiman. The common caiman is the best known and is the one commonly sold in pet stores.

The common caiman (the name caiman is of Carib Indian origin) ranges from Venezuela and the Guianas southward through the Amazon Basin. It is found on Trinidad and some other islands off the northern coast of South America. This species, whose maximum length is said to be eight and one-half feet, though most specimens are much smaller, occurs in a variety of habitats: ponds, lakes, swamps, marshes, streams, and occasionally a saltmarsh. It is found more often in still water than in flowing streams and is more common in open areas than in shaded places.

The caiman looks so much like an alligator that it is not necessary to describe it. Unlike the alligator, it does not have a bony septum between the nostrils, and it has a ventral armor composed of overlapping bony scutes, each formed of two parts united by a suture. Both the caiman and alligator differ from the crocodile in having the fourth lower tooth fitting into a socket instead of into a notch in the upper jaw as in the crocodile. There are other differences, too.

It is not known exactly what the common caiman eats in the wild, though it probably feeds on fish and various small aquatic organisms. Captive specimens forage like small alligators, rubbing the side of the snout over the substratum and biting at any food that they come across. They also use other senses to locate food.

The female builds her nest, often with vegetable debris scraped from the surface of the ground, usually no more than three feet from the edge of the water. The nest varies in size. If there is an abundance of loose material she may pile it into a good-sized nest. Damp finely divided material is usually formed into a small, tightly compacted nest. Sometimes the nest is constructed in full sunlight, but as a rule it is built in a thicket or beneath bushes and trees. If in the open, it may consist of fresh, green material.

It is generally believed that the female will not defend her nest. The common caiman is naturally shy and will escape into the water upon the approach of an intruder; however a large female will defend the nest even against humans.

When the nest has been completed the female may not immediately lay her eggs if the climatic conditions are not especially favorable but will wait until such time as they are. A clutch usually contains from twenty-five to thirty eggs. The smallest known clutch contained eighteen eggs and the largest forty. The size of the eggs varies in length from about one and three-quarters to two and three-quarters inches and in diameter from about one inch to one-and-one-half inches. Sometimes an egg is blunter and larger at one end than at the other, which is unusual among crocodilians. At the time of laying the shell is white, but it soon becomes stained by the debris of the nest. A few days after the eggs have been laid a whitish opaque band appears around the smaller circumference.

The hatchlings are about six inches long and are yellowish or yellowish-brown with black crossbands. There may be six

106

Fig. 40   Caiman

crossbands on the body and seven on the tail. They are often broken or incomplete. Sometimes the crossbands are present on only one side of the body (Fig. 40). A young captive baby caiman or juvenile may not cry out when taken hold of by its keeper, but in the wild, when seized by a predator and physically hurt, it will give voice to a distress call.

The natural enemies of the common caiman are not known but humans are probably its worst enemy. Each year thousands of hatchlings are shipped to the United States to be sold as pets or are mounted for sale as curios. And yet the caiman seems to hold its own in fair numbers because it is able to live in a variety of aquatic habitats and to subsist on a variety of small animals.

The young caiman should be kept in a semi-aquatic terrarium which should be fairly large to give the animal enough room to move about. The water in the aquarium should be at least three inches deep, so that the caiman can submerge itself completely, and the beach be large enough so that the animal can walk ashore when it so desires. Most important of all, the temperature should range from 75 to 95 degrees Fahrenheit. Part of the terrarium should have direct sunlight for an hour or two a day, but care must be exercised so that the terrarium doesn't get too hot. Excessive heat will kill your pet.

The caiman may be given a diet of fresh raw fish, earthworms, raw beef, and liver. Remember, it likes to take its food by sideswipes, so feed it from one side. At first the food may have to be forced into the animal's mouth. Add concentrated cod-liver oil to the diet. Three good feedings a week should be enough.

Appendix

Scientific Names of Reptiles Mentioned in This Book

Common Name	Scientific Name	Family
(Eastern) garter snake	*Thamnophis sirtalis sirtalis*	Colubridae
Gila monster	*Heloderma suspectum*	Helodermatidae
Mexican beaded lizard	*Heloderma horridum*	Helodermatidae
Blue-tailed skink	*Eumeces laticeps*	Scincidae
American alligator	*Alligator mississipiensis*	Crocodylidae
Chinese alligator	*Alligator sinensis*	Crocodylidae
Fence swift	*Sceloporus undulatus*	Iguanidae
Striped mud turtle	*Kinosternon bauri*	Chelydridae
Common mud turtle	*Kinosternon subrum*	Chelydridae
Leatherback turtle	*Dermochelys coriacea*	Dermochelidae
Yellow mud turtle	*Kinosternon flavescens*	Chelydridae
Reticulate python	*Python reticulatus*	Boidae
King cobra	*Naja hannah*	Elapidae
Eastern diamondback rattlesnake	*Crotalus adamanteus*	Viperidae

Komodo dragon	*Varanus komodoensis*	Varanidae
Common iguana	*Iguana iguana*	Iguanidae
Glass lizard	*Ophisaurus ventralis*	Anguidae
Congo dwarf crocodile	*Osteolaemus osborni*	Crocodylidae
Salt-water crocodile	*Crocodylus porosus*	Crocodylidae
American crocodile	*Crocodylus acutus*	Crocodylidae
Banded sand snake	*Chilomeniscus cinctus*	Colubridae
Horned rattlesnake	*Crotalus cerastes*	Viperidae
European common lizard	*Lacerta vivipara*	Lacertidae
Marine iguana	*Amblyrhynchus cristatus*	Iguanidae
Florida swamp snake	*Liodytes alleni*	Colubridae
Queen snake	*Natrix septemvittata*	Colubridae
Red-bellied snake	*Storeria occipitomaculata*	Colubridae
Chuckwalla	*Sauromalus obesus*	Iguanidae
Leopard lizard	*Gambelia wislizenii*	Iguanidae
Painted turtle	*Chrysemys picta*	Testudinidae
Western skink	*Eumeces skiltonianus*	Scincidae
Tornier's tortoise	*Malacochersus tornieri*	Testudinidae

Common snapping turtle	*Chelydra serpentina*	Chelydridae
Indian python	*Python molurus*	Boidae
Smooth green snake	*Opheodrys vernalis*	Colubridae
Bullsnake	*Pituophis melanoleucus sayi*	Colubridae
Green anole	*Anolis carolinensis carolinensis*	Iguanidae
Northern fence lizard	*Sceloporus undulatus hyacinthinus*	Iguanidae
Texas horned lizard	*Phrynosoma cornutum*	Iguanidae
Six-lined Race runner	*Cnemidophorus sexlineatus*	Teiidae
Western collared lizard	*Crotaphytus collaris baileyi*	Iguanidae
Red-eared turtle	*Pseudemys scripta elegans*	Testudinidae
Spotted turtle	*Clemmys guttata*	Testudinidae
Rubber boa	*Charina bottae*	Boidae
Hog-nosed snake	*Heterodon platyrhinos*	Colubridae
Wood turtle	*Clemmys insculpta*	Testudinidae
Striped ground uta	*Uta stansburiana stejnegeri*	Iguanidae
Alligator snapping turtle	*Macroclemys temmincki*	Chelydridae
Hawksbill turtle	*Eretmochelys imbricata*	Cheloniidae

Eastern box turtle	*Terrapene carolina carolina*	Testudinidae
Gulf Coast box turtle	*Terrapene carolina major*	Testudinidae
Florida Box Turtle	*Terrapene carolina bauri*	Testudinidae
Three-toed box turtle	*Terrapene carolina triunguis*	Testudinidae
Ornate box turtle	*Terrapene ornata ornata*	Testudinidae
Common musk turtle	*Sternothaerus odoratus*	Chelydridae
Carolina anole	*Anolis carolinensis*	Iguanidae
Eastern collared lizard	*Crotaphytus collaris*	Iguanidae
Reticulate collared lizard	*Crotaphytus reticulatus*	Iguanidae
Southern fence lizard	*Sceloporus undulatus undulatus*	Iguanidae
Five-lined skink	*Eumeces fasciatus*	Iguanidae
Eastern glass lizard	*Ophisaurus ventralis*	Anguidae
Island glass lizard	*Ophisaurus compressus*	Anguidae
Green grass snake	*Opheodrys vernalis*	Colubridae
Northern brown snake	*Storeria dekayi dekayi*	Colubridae
Northern water snake	*Natrix sipedon sipedon*	Colubridae

Ring-necked snake	*Diadophis punctatus edwardsii*	Colubridae
Eastern hog-nosed snake	*Heterodon platyrhinos*	Colubridae
Black caiman	*Melanosuchus niger*	Alligatoridae
Broad-nosed caiman	*Caiman latirostris*	Alligatoridae
Smooth-fronted caiman	*Paleosuchus trigonatus*	Alligatoridae
Dwarf caiman	*Paleosuchus palpebrosus*	Alligatoridae
Spectacled caiman	*Caiman sclerops*	Alligatoridae
Brown caiman	*Caiman sclerops fuscus*	Alligatoridae
Apoporis River caiman	*Caiman sclerops apaporiensis*	Alligatoridae
Paraguay Caiman	*Caiman sclerops yacare*	Alligatoridae
Common caiman	*Caiman sclerops sclerops*	Alligatoridae

Addresses of the Fish and Wildlife Service District Law Enforcement Offices

If You Reside In:	Please Write To: (Special Agent in Charge) U.S. Fish and Wildlife Service
Alaska	813 D Street Anchorage, Alaska 99501
Hawaii, Idaho, Oregon, or Washington	P.O. Box 3737 Portland, Oregon 97208
California or Nevada	Room E 2911 2800 Cottage Way Sacramento, California 95825
Colorado, Montana, Utah, or Wyoming	P.O. Box 25486 Denver Federal Center Denver, Colorado 80225
Iowa, Kansas, Missouri, Nebraska, North Dakota, or South Dakota	P.O. Box 1038 Independence, Missouri 64051
Arizona, New Mexico, Oklahoma, or Texas	P.O. Box 329 Albuquerque, New Mexico 87103
Illinois, Indiana, Michigan, Minnesota, Ohio, or Wisconsin	P.O. Box 45 Twin Cities, Minnesota 55111
Arkansas, Louisiana, or Mississippi	546 Carondelet Street Room 408 New Orleans, Louisiana 70130

Alabama, Florida, Georgia, Puerto Rico, or Virgin Islands	P.O. Box 95467 Atlanta, Georgia 30347
Kentucky, North Carolina, South Carolina, or Tennessee	P.O. Box 290 Nashville, Tennessee 37202
Delaware, Maryland, District of Columbia, Pennsylvania, Virginia, or West Virginia	95 Aquahart Road Glen Burnie, Maryland 21061
New Jersey or New York	Century Bank Bldg. 2nd Floor 700 Rockaway Turnpike Lawrence, New York 11559
Connecticut, Maine, Massachusetts, New Hampshire, Rhode Island, or Vermont	P.O. Box 34 Boston, Massachusetts 02101

ANIMAL DEALERS AND SUPPLY HOUSES

Alligator Farm—P. O. Drawer E., St. Augustine, Florida 32084

Armstrong Cricket Farm—Glenville, Georgia 30427

Bannerman Reptile Supply—P. O. Box 2462, Tallahassee, Florida 32304

Carolina Biological Supply Company—Burlington, North Carolina 27215

Frisky Bait Service—291 Watertown Street, Newton, Massachusetts 02158

Fulmer Cricket Farm—2012 Roosevelt Drive, Augusta, Georgia 30900

Hermosa Reptile and Wild Animal Farm—P. O. Box 182, Hermosa, California 90254

Herpetofauna International—207 Davisville Road, Willow Grove, Pennsylvania 19090

Hurst, Robert—Route 6 Box 30, Slidell, Louisiana 70458

Lucky Lure Cricket Farm—Leesburg, Florida 32748

De Melo, Joseph, Exotic Kingdom—6207 Vermillion Boulevard, New Orleans, Louisiana 70122

Midwest Reptile Company—720 Colerick Street, Ft. Wayne, Indiana 46806

Newsom's Varmits 'N' Things—5220 Airline, Houston, Texas 77022

Philadelphia Reptile Exchange—436 Vernon Street, Jenkintown, Pennsylvania 19046

Picheo's Reptile Gardens—Rt. 2 Box 251, Pensacola, Florida 32506

Rainbow Mealworms—126 E. Spruce Street, Compton, California 90220

Roth, Bob—Route 4 Box 241, Ft. Pierce, Florida 33450

Snake Farm—P. O. Box 96, LaPlace, Louisiana 70068

Southwestern Herpetological Sales—P. O. Box 282, Calimessa, California 92320

Wild Cargo—520 North Dixie Highway, Hollywood, Florida 33022

Bibliography

Babcock, H. *Turtles of the Northeastern United States*. New York: Dover Publications, Inc., 1971.

Carr, A.F., *Handbook of Turtles*. Ithaca, New York: Comstock Publishing Associates, 1952.

Colbert, E.H. *The Age of Reptiles*. New York: W.W. Norton & Company, Inc., 1965.

Conant, R. *A Field Guide to Reptiles and Amphibians*. Boston: Houghton Mifflin Company, 1958.

Ditmars, R.L. *The Reptiles of North America*. New York: Doubleday, Doran and Company, 1940.

Minton, S.A. and Minton, M.R. *Giant Reptiles*. New York: Charles Scribner's Sons, 1973.

Neill, W.T. *The Last of the Ruling Reptiles*. New York: Columbia University Press, 1971.

Oliver, J.A. *The Natural History of North American Amphibians and Reptiles*. Princeton: D.Van Nostrand Company, Inc., 1955.

Parker, H.W. *Snakes of the World*. New York: Dover Publications, Inc., 1963.

Pope, C.H. *The Reptile World*. New York: Alfred A. Knopf, 1966.

Schmidt, K.P. and Davis, D.D. *Field Book of Snakes*. New York: G.P. Putnam's Sons, 1941.

Smith, H.M. *Handbook of Lizards*. Ithaca, New York: Comstock Publishing Company, 1946.

Stebbins, R.C. *A Field Guide of Western Reptiles and Amphibians*. Boston: Houghton Mifflin Company, 1966.

Van Denburgh, J. *The Reptiles of Western North America*, Vol. 1 *Lizards*; Vol. 2 *Snakes and Turtles*. San Francisco: California Academy of Sciences, 1922.

Wright, A.H. and Wright, A.A. *Handbook of Snakes*. Ithaca, New York: Comstock Press, 1957.

Index